Claudia Molitor

Sonorama

Listening to the view from the train

Uniformbooks 2015

First published 2015
Uniformbooks in partnership with Electra
www.electra-productions.com

ISBN 978-1-910010-03-7
Photography by Lucy Dawkins
Copy editing by Amber Priestley and Ash Reid

Uniformbooks
7 Hillhead Terrace, Axminster, Devon EX13 5JL
www.uniformbooks.co.uk

Printed and bound by T J International, Padstow, Cornwall

Contents

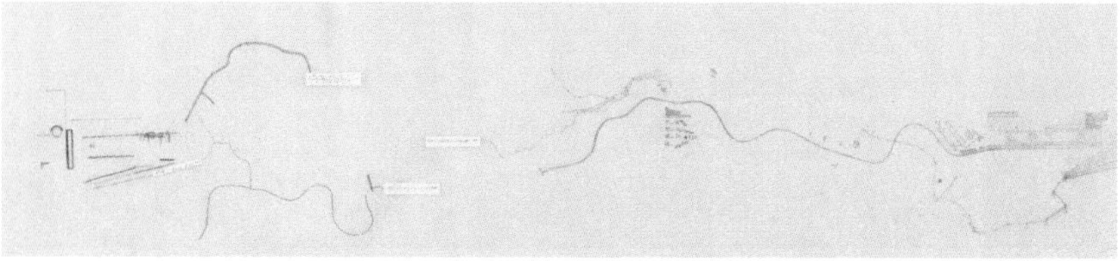
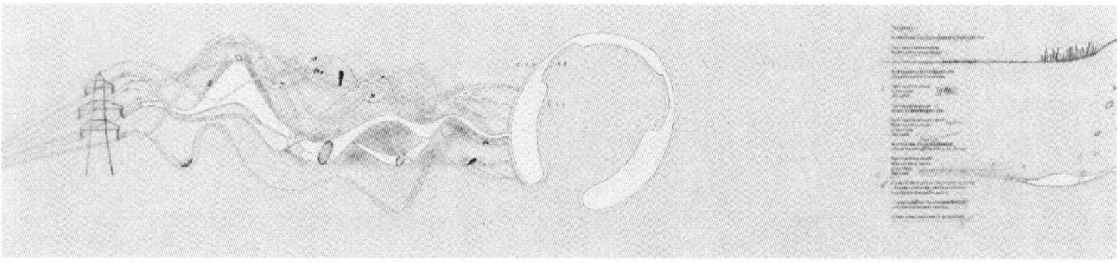
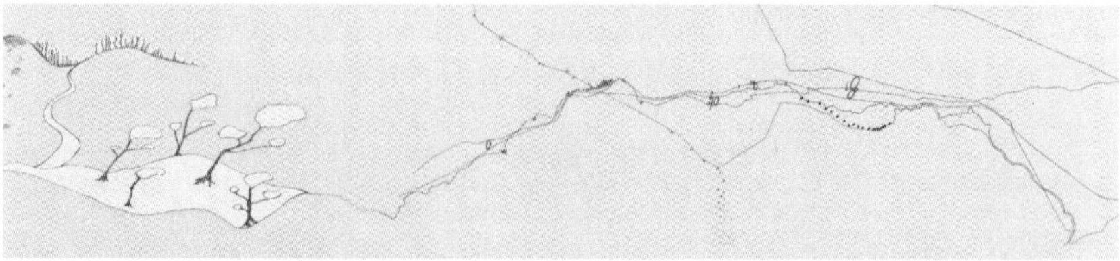
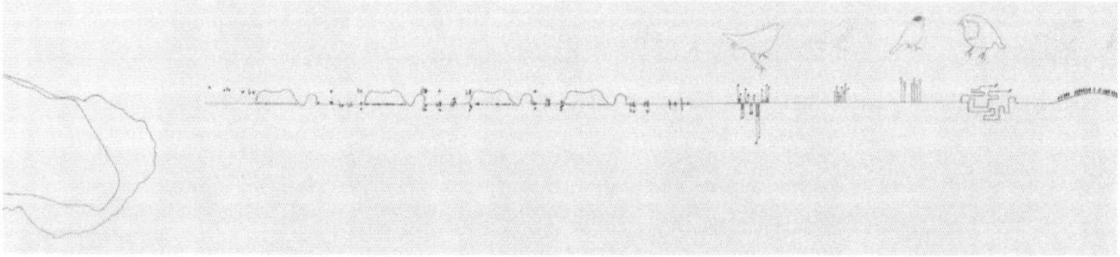

Sonorama

> "Transport... is distinguished not by the employment of mechanical means but by the dissolution of the intimate bond that, in wayfaring, couples locomotion and perception. The transported traveller becomes a passenger, who does not himself move but is rather moved from place to place. The sights, sounds and feelings that accost him during the passage have absolutely no bearing on the motion that carries him forth." [1]

In some way *Sonorama* is a challenge to this disconnect between the traveller and their journey. It suggests that the train carriage does not necessarily have to be a non-space which is endured in order to reach the desired destination, but that being in this moving space might be a meaningful experience in and of itself: an experience that could be approached as an opportunity to daydream, to ponder, to ruminate whilst gazing out of the window into the silently passing landscape. And, when you arrive, you might even be changed by your experience of travelling.

The landscape we see passing by between our station stops becomes a kind of in-between space to us. Stripped of its sounds as well as its smells and tactile sensations, it no longer touches us like a 'real' experienced space, but rather like a filmic space. By proposing a quasi-sonic reading of the passing view, the composed episodes of *Sonorama* liberate the outside space (outside the train carriage) from its in-between-ness, suggesting a possible re-establishment of a relationship between the landscape that is travelled through and us, the travellers. If the railroad represented a "...transformation of landscape into geographical space..." [2] when it first appeared, then perhaps *Sonorama*, through sound, will transform the traveller's experience of that geographical space into something approaching a landscape again.

During 2013 and 2014 I was doing a lot of long-distance commuting, spending at least 20 hours a week on a train. Travellers use this time in different ways, either filling it with activity or using it as a time-out from *doing*. I waver between the two, depending on what happens to be most pressing at the time. But primarily for me on such journeys a lot of productive thinking can happen whilst gazing out of the window. And I never tire of the sights: even on very familiar routes the sights are ever-changing. At some point during this time I became acutely aware, however, that the soundworld of my travelling seemed far more 'static' than the visual world—the humming of the train remaining relatively constant and drone-like. I am exaggerating of course; there is a lot of human sonic activity on most train journeys, nonetheless the visual space outside the carriage appears as an active, fast moving, film-like space, whereas the sound that goes with it, the sound of the train and the inside of the carriage, feels slower, inactive and somewhat stagnant.

If we so wish, we can shape this sonic space by listening to music or a podcast, and many of us do. The *listened* to does not, however, relate directly to anything we might be looking at. We make links and connections of course; we have imagination! But the music or podcast is not intended to relate to the particular landscape we happen to be passing.

So I started to wonder... what if I were to use a particular train route as the score for a work, where I would become the interpreter of this score by making an episodic work made of original compositions, field recordings, archive recordings, readings and conversations? A piece that could be listened to whilst travelling along this score, and importantly one that would relate specifically to that route. The experience of exactly how these episodes relate and the connections made between the heard and the seen would remain, of course, essentially with the listener. So that the looking and listening train traveller is the performer of the *Sonorama* and their experience of *looking* and *listening* the main focus of the work.

The starting point of the research was the map department at the British Library. The large Ordinance Survey maps were very useful to get a sense of the geography—and to some extent the human history—related to the route. And then there were inspiring old maps such as the ones from John Ogilby's 1675 *Britannia* Atlas.

Armed with this skeleton of information, the historian David Hendy and the sound archive curator Cheryl Tipp started digging out some fabulous nuggets from the British Library archives, which led to many happy hours listening and reading through material that in some way related to the route from St Pancras to Margate.

There were pertinent contemporary concerns too: the consumer capitalist heaven/hell at Stratford International, fed partly by the enormous new Port of London whose cranes can be glimpsed from the train as you pass through Ebbsfleet International; the negative attitude towards immigration that has reared its ugly head once again, and seems to forget the social and cultural enrichment that immigration brings. Indeed this seemed particularly relevant as the technology to travel allows cultures to intertwine, our perception to be altered and our experience to be expanded.

It was interesting to find the old Roman Road running alongside most of the journey and walk to Richborough near Sandwich with Charlotte Higgins; to read about the lives of the East London hop-pickers and discover that David Hendy himself picked hop in Kent as a student; to hear Evan Parker and Graham McKenzie talk about the danger of falling asleep on stage whilst performing with closed eyes; and to learn that Irene Revell had been a member of the 'Rail Riders' club for young fans of British Rail.

The architect Juhani Pallasmaa expresses about art and architecture what I envisaged the *Sonorama* to be and hope it has become:

> "Art articulates our existentially essential experiences, but... it also represents particular modes of thinking. Reactions to the world and processing of information take place directly as an embodied and sensory activity without being turned into concepts or even entering the sphere of consciousness."[3]

Claudia Molitor

---

1 Tim Ingold, *Lines: A Brief History* (Oxon/New York: Routledge, 2007) p.78.

2 Wolfgang Schivelbusch, *The Railway Journey: The Industrialization of Time and Space in the 19th Century* (Leamington Spa/Hamburg/New York: Berg Publishers, 1986) p.53.

3 Juhani Pallasmaa, *The Thinking Hand: Existential and Embodied Wisdom in Architecture* (Chichester: John Wiley & Sons, 2009) p.118.

THE SKETCH OF THE SCORE

Sonorama

Railway

> "...a complete bog of mud and filth with deep cart ruts, wretched hovels, the doors blocked up with mud, heaps of ashes, oyster shells and decayed vegetables. The stench is enough to knock down a bullock."

That's how Charles Dickens described the area around St Pancras.[1] Luckily the relatively new technology of the railroad offered a window of escape from this city malaise. Stepping on to a train at St Pancras could deliver you to the Kent coast with its endless skies and seaside delights in a matter of hours. But this wasn't without its dangers! Paul Farley and Michael Symmons Roberts explain that

> "There was a great fear of modern speed. Early railway travellers were anxious of the effects that those new velocities might have on their bodies, and it was speculated that cows in fields nearby a passing train would have their milk turned black. Even the long-distance horse coaches were considered dangerous: after completing the 400-mile journey to Edinburgh, Lord Campbell wrote how he had been 'gravely advised to stay a day at York, as several passengers who had gone through without stopping died of apoplexy from the rapidity of the motion'."[2]

Moreover, hurtling through the land was believed to lead to an annihilation of space and time; take Filippo Tommaso Marinetti's description of speed for example: "Speed destroys the laws of gravity. It makes time and space subjective, thereby enslaving them. For the fast man, kilometres and hours aren't identical. But rather variable in both length and duration."[3]

Technology certainly changes the way we understand our world; and if it was for some a threatening change, to others it was much more positive. The railroad could intertwine cultures, enrich our perceptions and expand our experience of the world, as Wolfgang Schivelbusch explains: "Jules Clariétie, a Parisian journalist and publicist, characterized the view from the train window as an evanescent landscape whose rapid motion made it possible to grasp the whole, to get an overview: defining the process, he made specific use of the concept of panorama: 'In a few hours, it [the railway] shows you all of France, and before your eyes it unrolls its infinite panorama, a vast succession of charming tableaux, of novel surprises. Of a landscape it shows you only the great outlines... Don't ask it for details, but for the living whole..."[4]

In 1836, Government too realised the potential of the railroad for connecting to cultures beyond our shores: "An Act for making a Railway from the London and Croydon Railway to Dover, to be called 'The South-eastern Railway' [21st June 1836]

> Whereas the making a Railway from the London and Croydon Railway, at the Termination thereof at Croydon, to Dover, would be productive of great Advantage, by opening an additional, certain, and expeditious Communication between the Metropolis and the Town of Tunbridge, the Weald of Kent and Dover, and other Towns and Districts on the South-eastern Coast, and also by facilitating the Communication between London and the Continent of Europe: And whereas the several Persons hereinafter named are willing, at their own Expense, to carry into execution the before-mentioned Undertaking, but the same cannot be effected without the Authority of Parliament: May it therefore please your Majesty that it may be enacted; and be it enacted by the King's most Excellent Majesty, by and with the Advice and Consent of the Lords Spiritual and Temporal, and Commons, in Parliament assembled, and by the Authority of the same..."

But let's not forget that, as with much development, 'progress' for some is often built on the plight and disadvantage of others.

"[...T]he navvy [or railway worker] has been the pioneer of every railway that we have." says the Rev. L. M. Evans writing in 1878 "And as now we pass in rapid travel from end to end of England over the smooth and level iron road, each embankment, every cutting, every tunnel, bridge and viaduct, yes, every foot of road bears witness to the hard and patient toil of many a thousand navvy hands. The navvies have been everywhere before us, and have passed on out of sight..." But they were certainly not celebrated as pioneers or explorers. Evans goes on to describe a conversation with a navvy:

> "Outlaws, sir, that's what we are. Wanderers on the face of the earth, and outcasts from the society of all decent people"

"Why, it was only t'other day as I heard a woman telling about a railway accident, and she said as there was three men killed and a *navvy*. That's the way, sir. We aint *men* at all, we aint got no feelings nor no soul, nor nothing but just string backs and arms and a big swallow for beer." [5]

1 Stephen Bayley, *Work: The Building of the Channel Tunnel Rail Link* (London & New York: Merrell, 2007) p.8.

2 Paul Farley and Michael Symmons Roberts, *Edgelands: Journeys into England's True Wilderness* (London: Vintage Books, 2012) p.103.

3 Filippo Tommaso Marinetti, translated by Jeffrey T. Schnapp, in J. T. Schnapp (ed.), *Speed Limits* (Skira Editione, 2009) p.257.

4 Wolfgang Schivelbusch, *The Railway Journey: The Industrialization of Time and Space in the 19th Century* (Leamington Spa/Hamburg/New York: Berg Publishers, 1986) p.61.

5 Rev. L. M. Evans, *Navvies and Their Needs* (1878) pp.4–8.

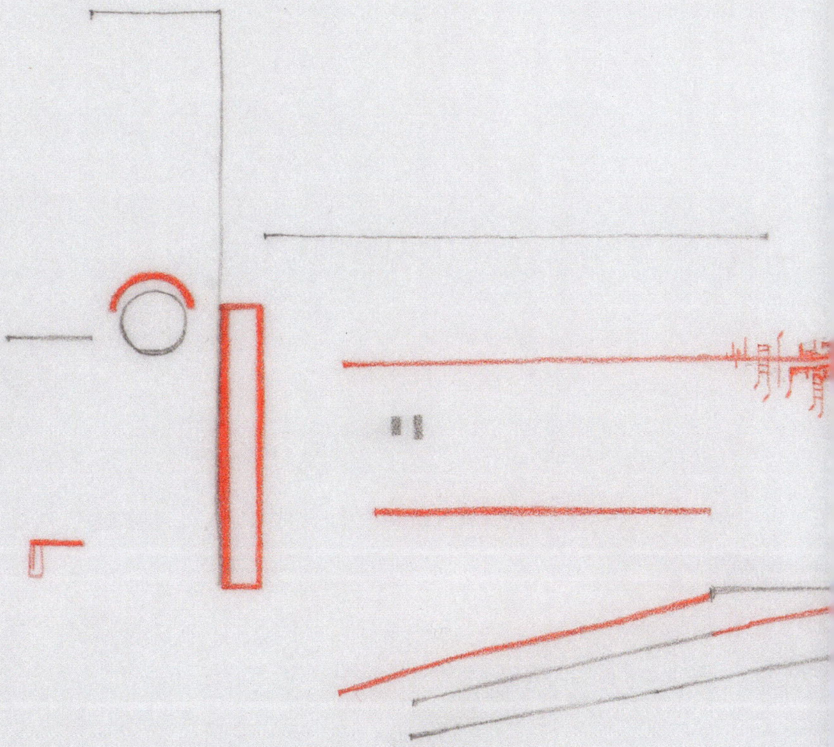

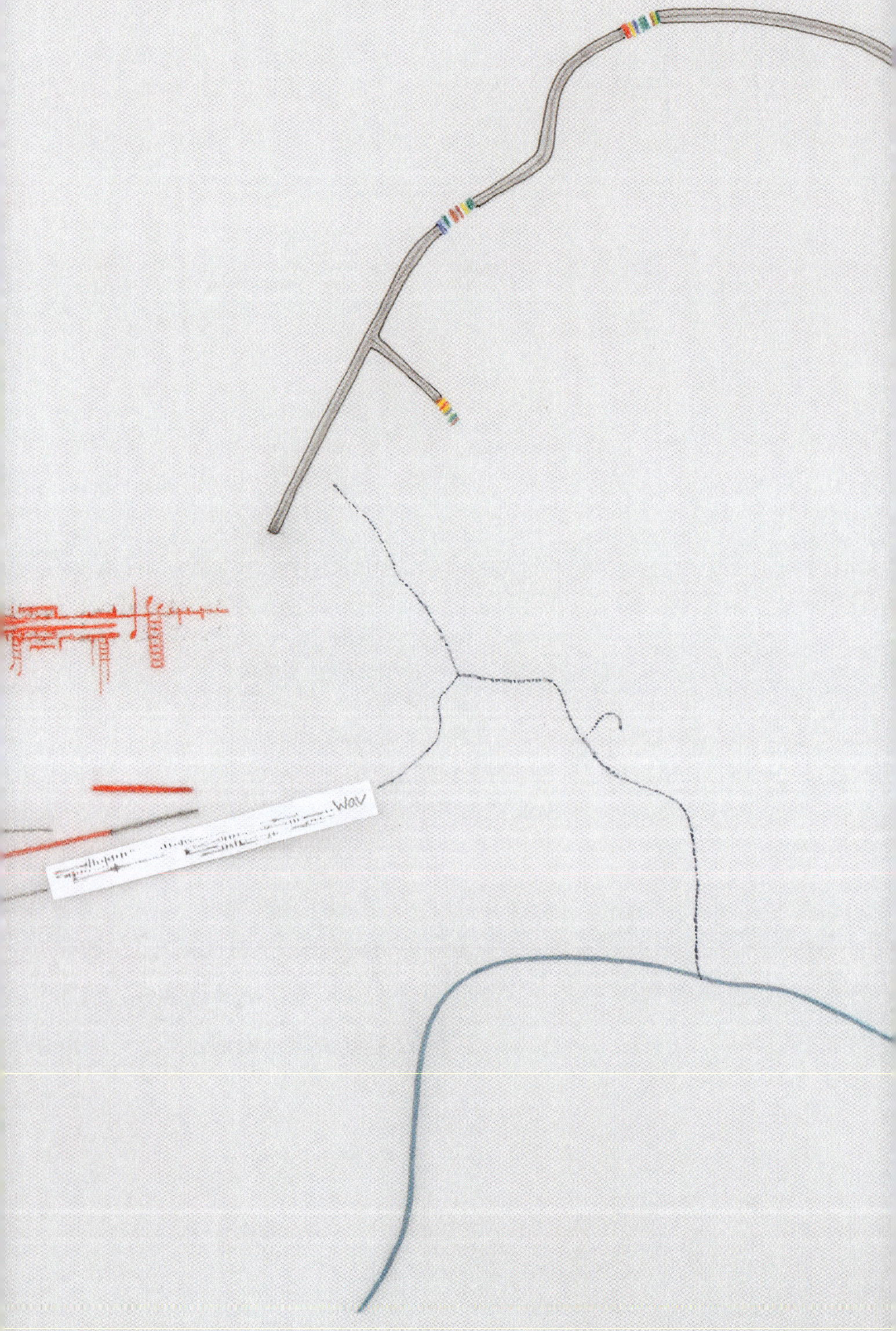
wav

wav

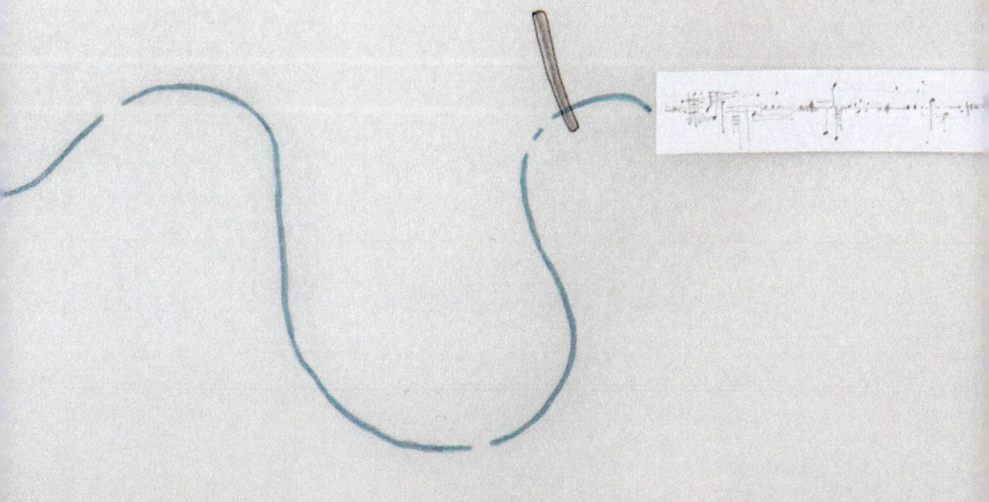

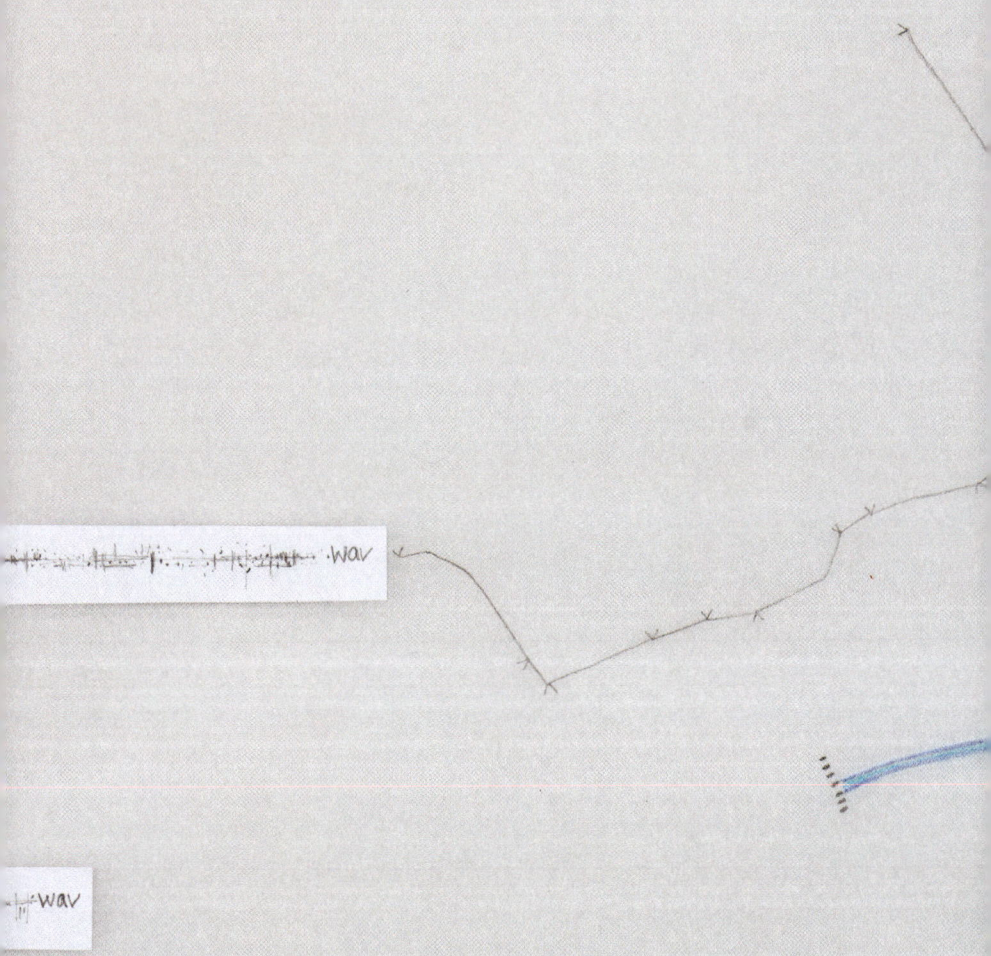
.wav
wav

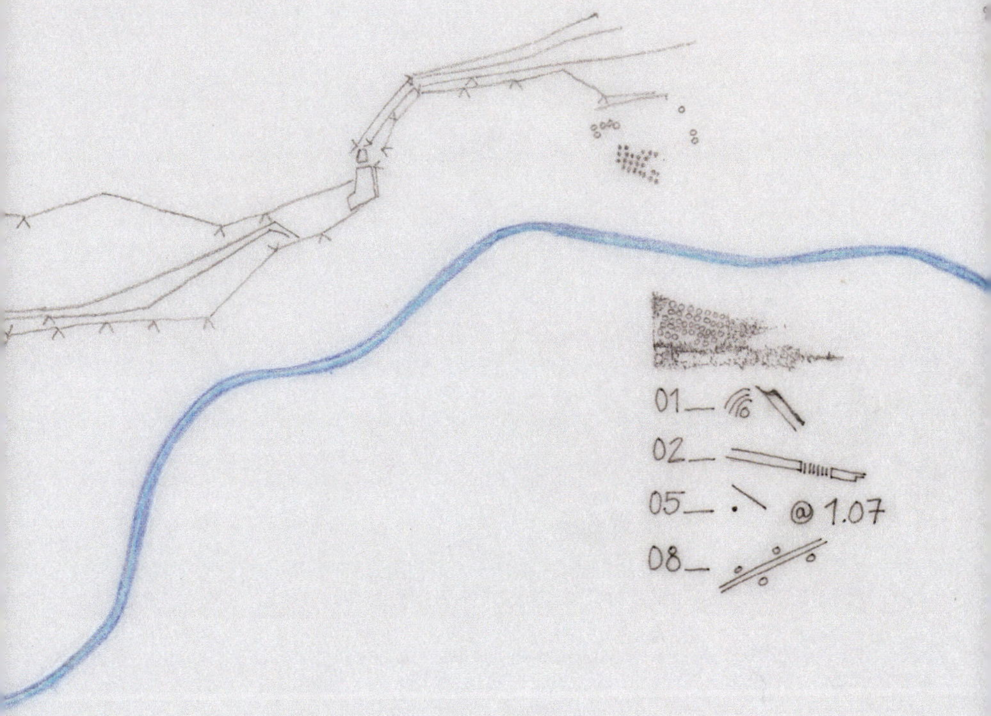
01_
02_
05_ @ 1.07
08_

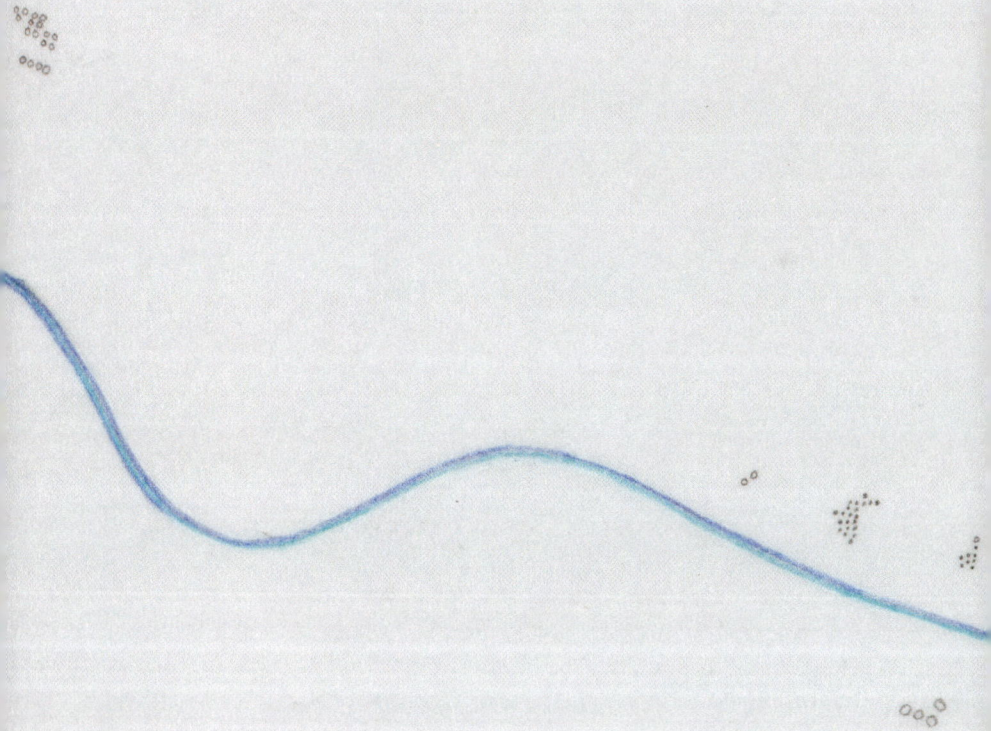

Journeying

"Lost really has two disparate meanings. Losing things is about the familiar falling away, getting lost is about the unfamiliar appearing. There are objects and people that disappear from your sight or knowledge or possession; you lose a bracelet, a friend, the key. You still know where you are. Everything is familiar except that there is one item less, one missing element. Or you get lost, in which case the world has become larger than your knowledge of it. Either way, there is a loss of control. Imagine yourself streaming through time shedding gloves, umbrellas, wrenches, books, friends, homes, names. This is what the view looks like if you take a rear-facing seat on the train. Looking forward you constantly acquire moments of arrival, moments of realization, moments of discovery. The wind blows your hair back and you are greeted by what you have never seen before. The material falls away in onrushing experience. It peels off like skin from a molting snake. Of course to forget the past is to lose the sense of loss that is also memory of an absent richness and a set of clues to navigate the present by: the art is not one of forgetting but letting go. And when everything else is gone, you can be rich in loss."[1] writes Rebecca Solnit, *A Field Guide to Getting Lost.*

Once you have stepped onto a train you can't very easily get lost, but you do lose control of your locomotion through space. In fact the journey of a traveller is a very different experience to that of the wayfarer, as the anthropologist Tim Ingold explains:

> "The wayfarer is continually on the move. More strictly, he is his movement.
>
> .
>
> For the Inuit, as [Claudio] Aporta observes, "life happens while travelling. Other travellers are met, children are born, and hunting, fishing and other subsistence activities are performed…"
>
> .
>
> Unlike wayfaring… transport is destination-oriented. It is not so much a development *along* a way of life as a carrying *across*, from location to location, of people and goods in such a way as

> to leave their basic natures unaffected. Even the wayfarer, of course, goes from place to place... He must periodically pause to rest, and may even return repeatedly to the same abode... Each pause, however, is a moment of tension that—like holding one's breath—becomes ever more intense and less sustainable the longer it lasts. Indeed the wayfarer... has no final destination, for wherever he is, and as long as life goes on, there is somewhere further he can go. For the transported traveller and his baggage, by contrast, every destination is a terminus, every port a point of re-entry into a world from which he has been temporarily exiled whilst in transit. This point marks a moment not of tension but of completion.
>
> .
>
> Transport... is distinguished not by the employment of mechanical means but by the dissolution of the intimate bond that, in wayfaring, couples locomotion and perception. The transported traveller becomes a passenger, who does not himself move but is rather moved from place to place. The sights, sounds and feelings that accost him during the passage have absolutely no bearing on the motion that carries him forth."[2]

Gazing out from inside the train carriage we experience a constantly evolving panorama, but its soundworld lies silent behind the window glass. This does not necessarily strike us as odd in our contemplation of a landscape. Since the early 19th century the spectacle of the panoramic view has captivated our imagination. Experiencing a 'stunning' view is believed to have the capacity to deeply affect us, to contain profound meaning, from which we will emerge changed, even enlightened. These views, however, are mostly thought of as silent, or at least quiet, with only a gentle, trickling soundtrack such as lapping waves or bubbling streams. And when we move through a land—or city—scape on a train, the act of doing so *silences* that passing view for us sat in the carriage completely as the train thunders along its tracks.

But gazing out of the window, listening to words and music, contemplating sounds and sites, and maybe most of all daydreaming might allow you to just recapture some of that sense of connectedness to your journey through time... or feel like the poet Rainer Maria Rilke did about travelling as he wrote to a friend:

> "Oh, the joys of travel! To feel the excitement of sudden departure, not always knowing whither. Surely you and I are in agreement about that. How often did my life seem concentrated in that single moment of departure. To travel

far, far—and that first morning's awakening under a new sky! And to find oneself in it—no, to discover more of oneself there. To experience there, too, where one has never been before, one's own continuity of being and, at the same time, to feel that something in your heart, somehow indigenous to this new land, is coming to life from the moment of your arrival. You feel your blood infused with some new intelligence, wondrously nourished by things you had no way of knowing."[3]

1 Rebecca Solnit, *A Field Guide to Getting Lost* (Edinburgh: Canongate Books, 2006) pp.22–23.

2 Tim Ingold, *Lines: A Brief History* (Oxon/New York: Routledge, 2007) pp.77–88.

3 Rainer Maria Rilke, in a letter to a friend, 3 February 1923.

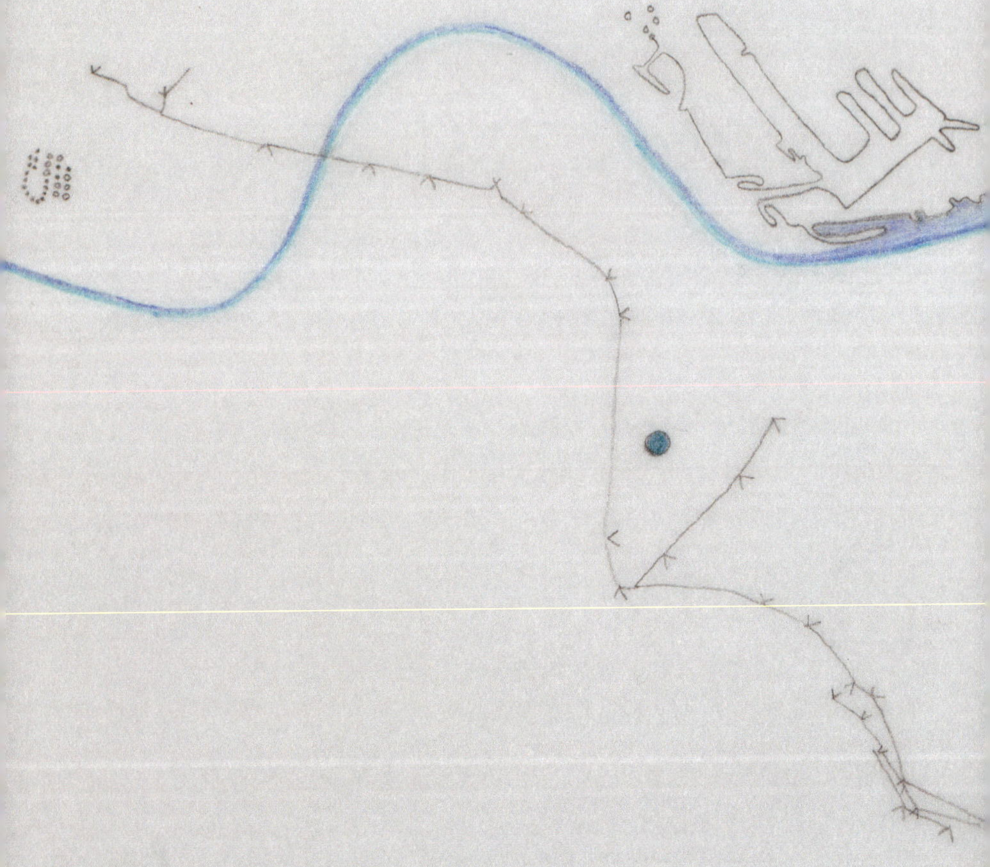

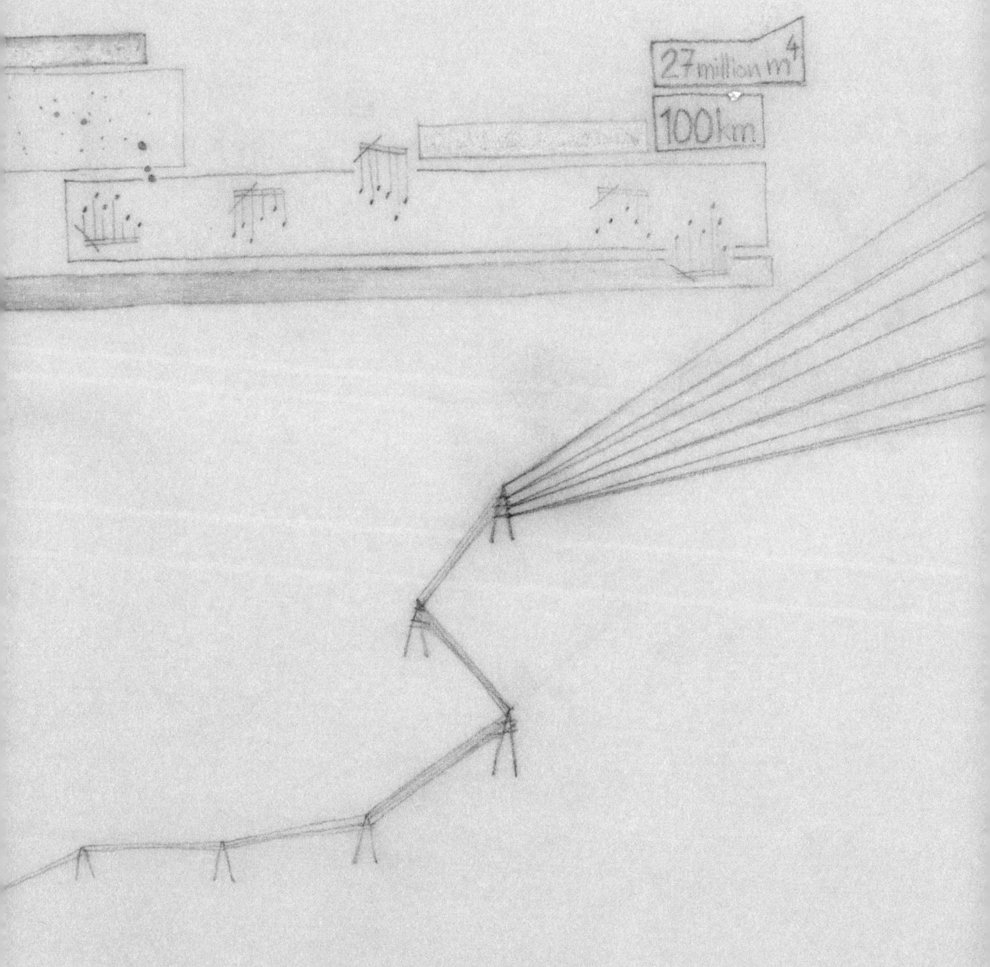
27 million m4
100km

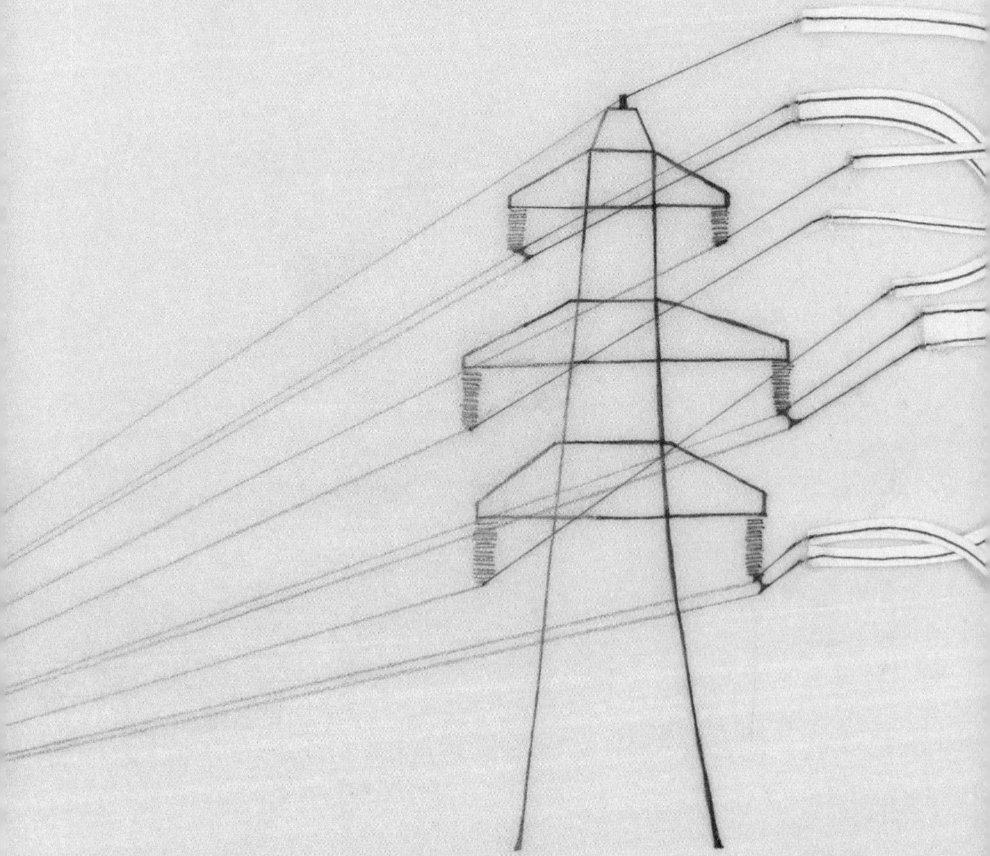

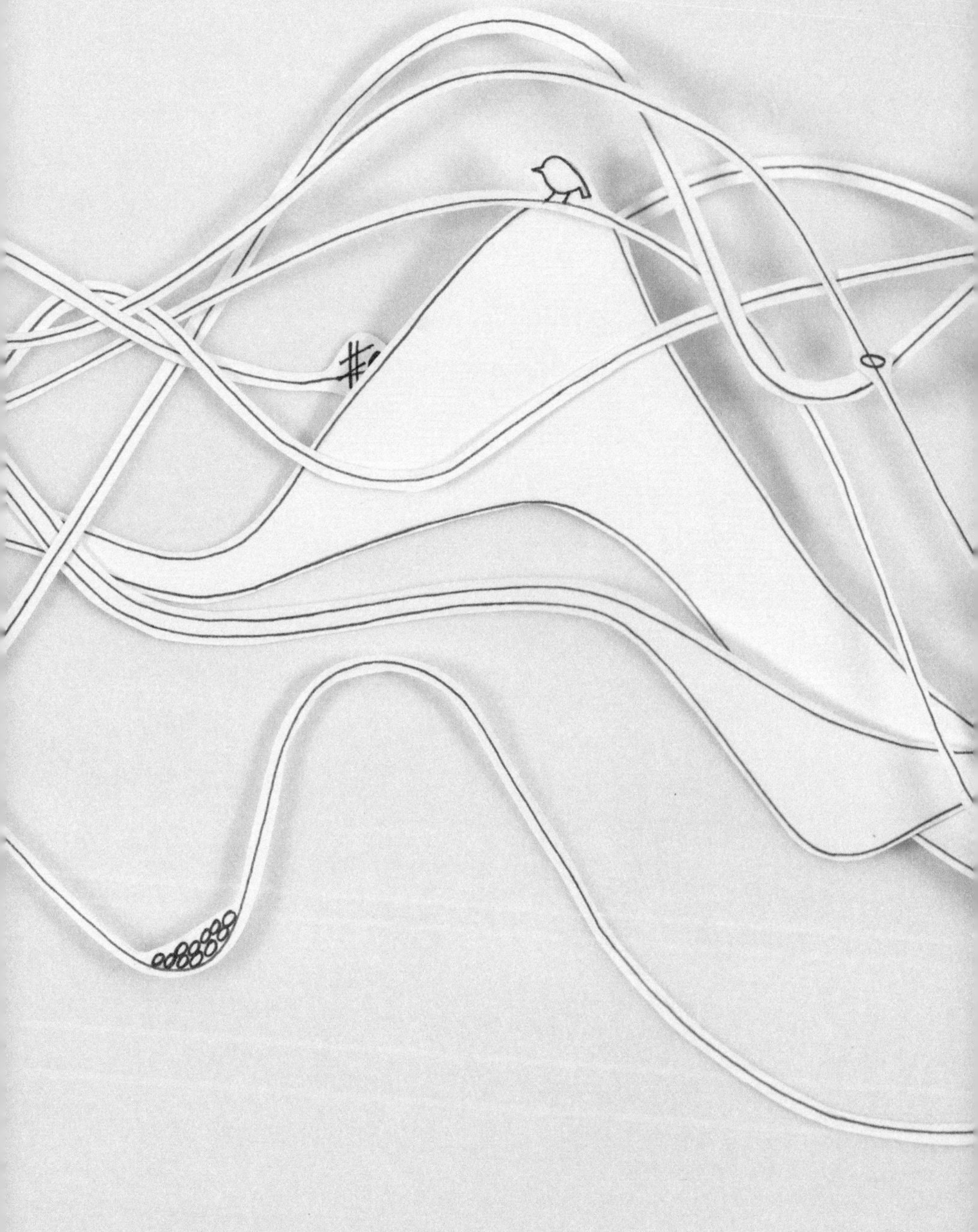

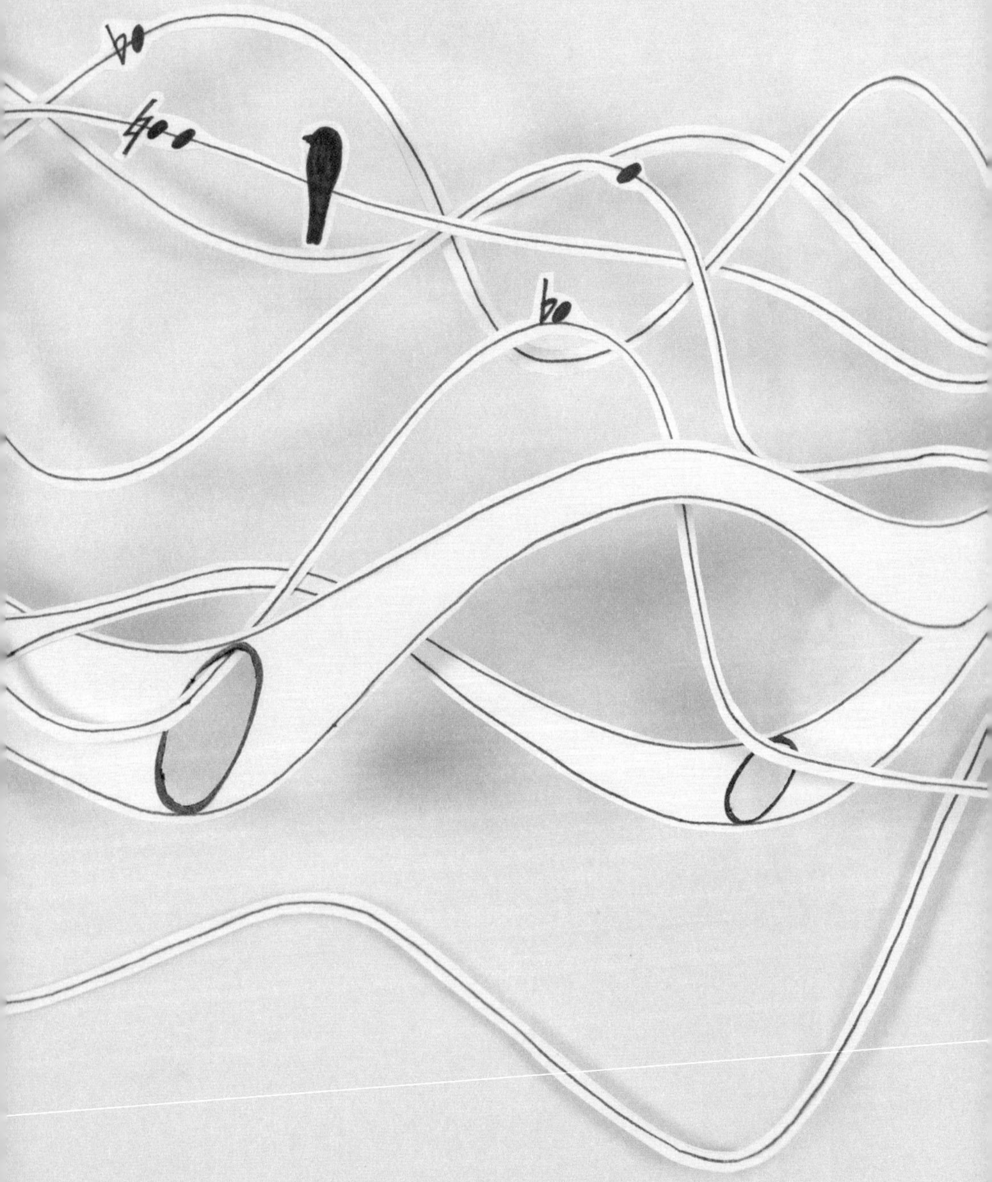

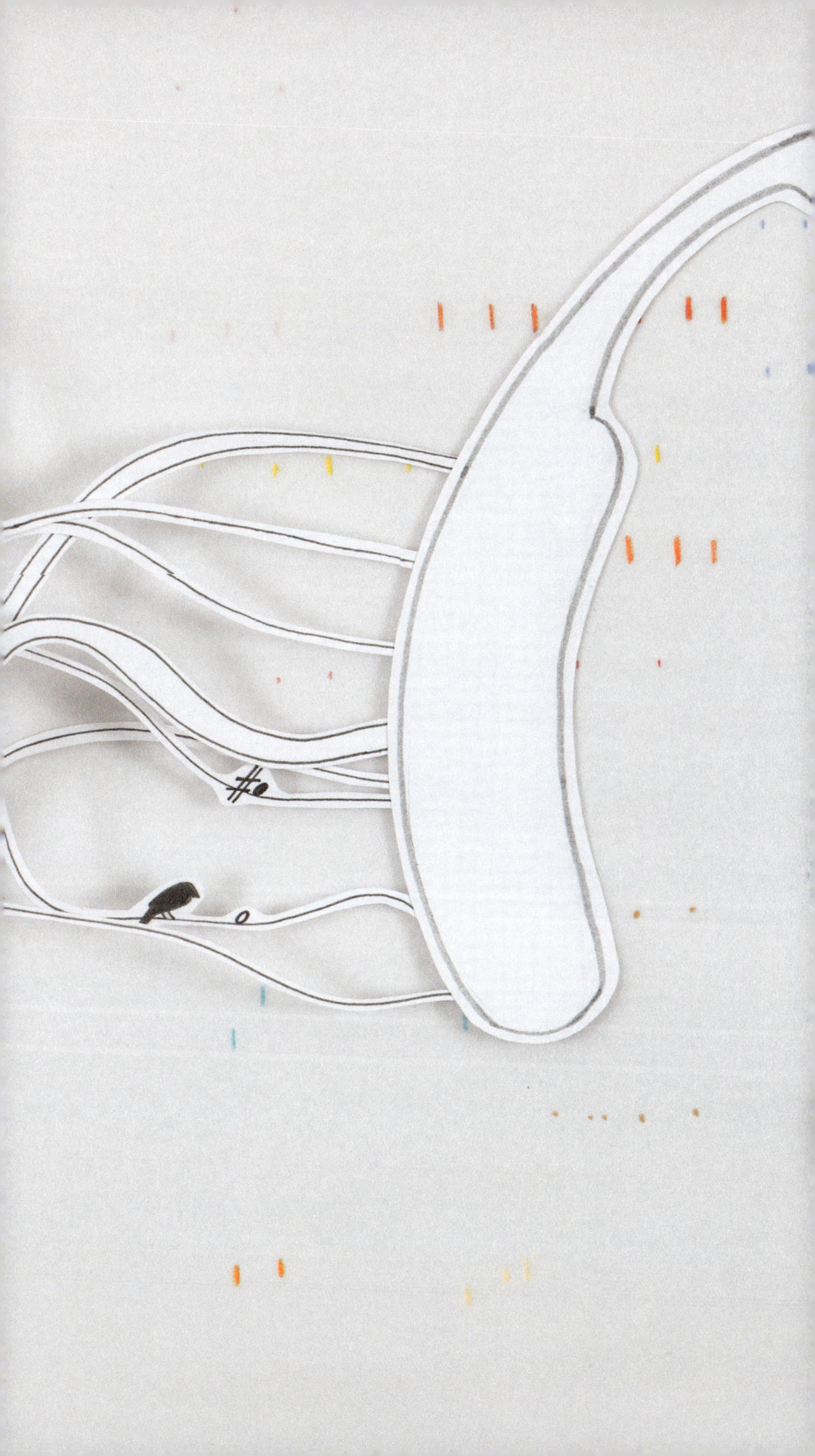

Hop picking

What we observe, how something appears to us when rushing past it on the train can gives us a warped view on the realities of what we are seeing. Take Bradshaw's description of the Kentish hop plantations:

> "...We next pass through a hop-plantation, and in summer when the vine has swung up to the top of the poles, and the shoots have thrust themselves off to the next, and so joined in a leafy communion of luxuriant vegetation, the scene becomes truly Arcadian..."[1]

But there is nothing particularly pastorally idyllic or harmonious about hop-picking. In his 'Hop-Picking Diaries' from 1913, George Orwell describes life working in the Kentish fields:

> "The most successful pitches are families, who have two or three adults to strip the vines, and a couple of children to pick up the fallen hops and clear the odd strands. The laws about child labour are disregarded utterly, and some of the people drive their children pretty hard... But they like the work and I don't suppose it did them more harm than school.
>
> Most of us slept in round tin huts... with no glass in the windows, and all kinds of holes to let in the wind and rain... The water tap was 200 yards away, and the latrine the same distance, but it was so filthy that one would have walked a mile sooner than use it. There was a stream where one could do some laundering, but getting a bath in the village would have been about as easy as buying a tame whale.
>
> There were uproarious scenes in the village on Saturdays, for the people who had money used to get well drunk... I have no doubt the residents thought us a nasty vulgar lot, but I could not help feeling that it was rather good for a dull village to have this invasion of cockneys once a year."[2]

1 John Christopher and Simon Jeffs (eds.), *Bradshaw's Guide: Vol.4: South Eastern Railway: London, Chatham & Dover* (Stroud: Amberley, 2014) p.24.

2 George Orwell in Peter Davison (ed.), *The Orwell Diaries* (London: Penguin Books, 2009) p.11–17.

Visiocentric

1 Subterranean histories embedded in the background

Your disconnected hearing
might listen at the landscape

Sonic erosions are gathering ~~inside the carriage~~

Your constantly evolving panorama
lays silent behind that window

2 *What we aim to create*
Is not simply
But rather

The passing landscape
shapes my ~~travelling~~ thoughts

And I consider the sonic afresh
What we aim to create
together
Is not simply
But rather

simultaneous

Your dialogue of seeing hearing ~~an hearing~~
follows me through the sites of this journey

New sounds are diluted
What we aim to create
Is not simply
But rather

3 spoken

It is for all these reasons that I remain unnerved
... looking out onto the view from this train
--- audible and inaudible instants

... listening ~~out~~ into the view ~~from this train~~
--- visible and invisible incidents

is there a sonic equivalent to picturesque?
spoken

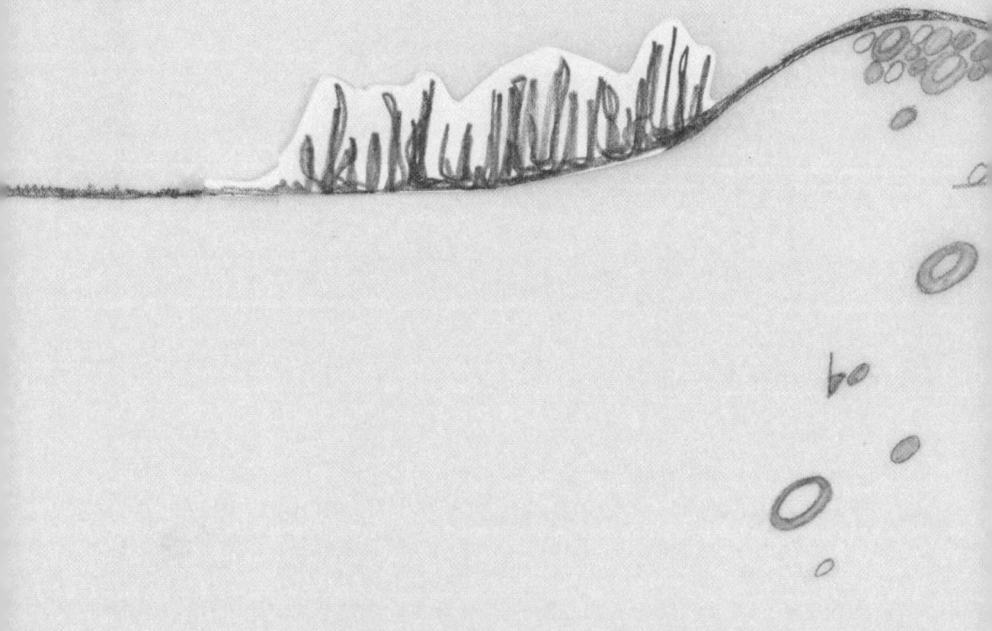
40

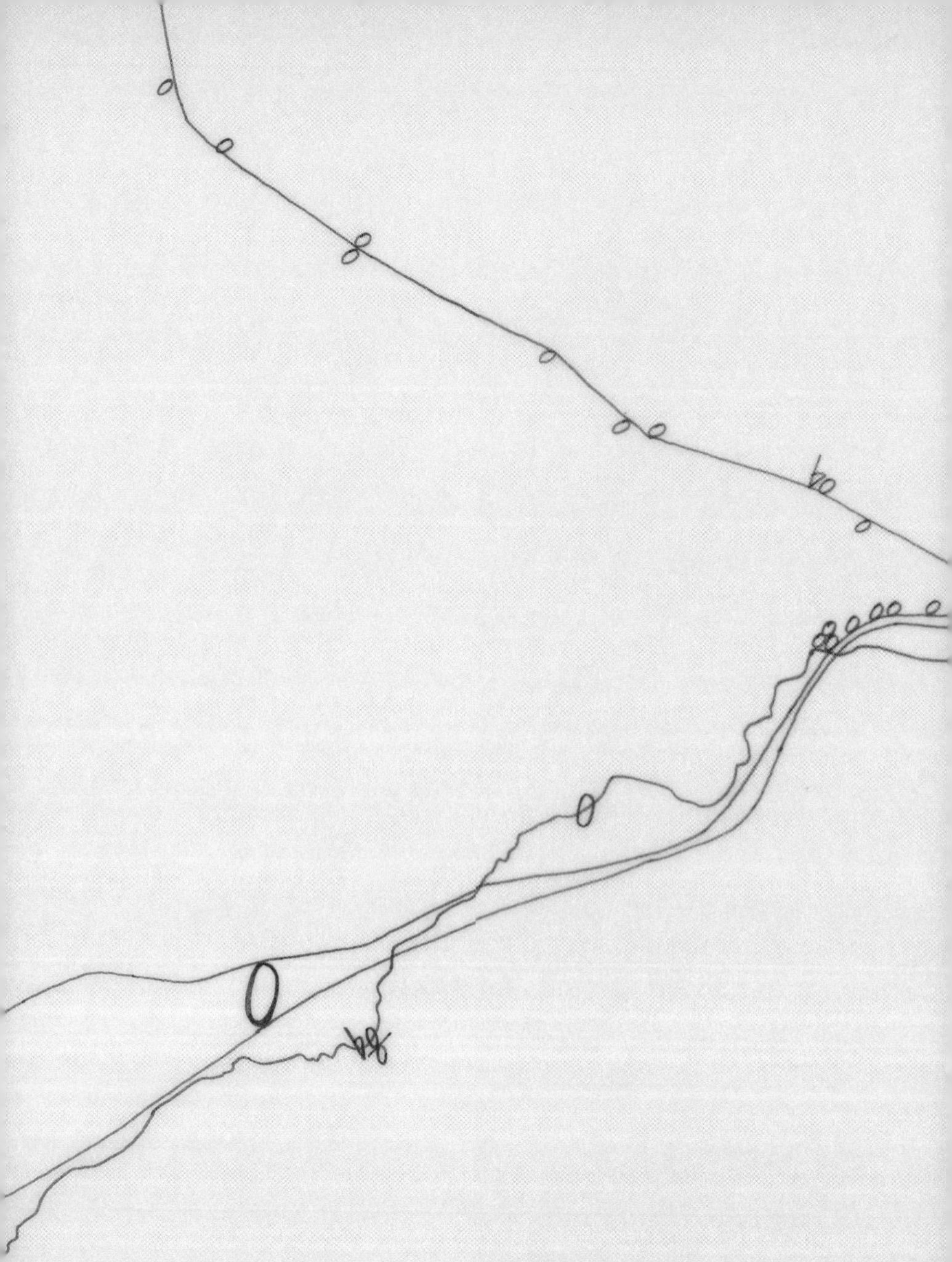

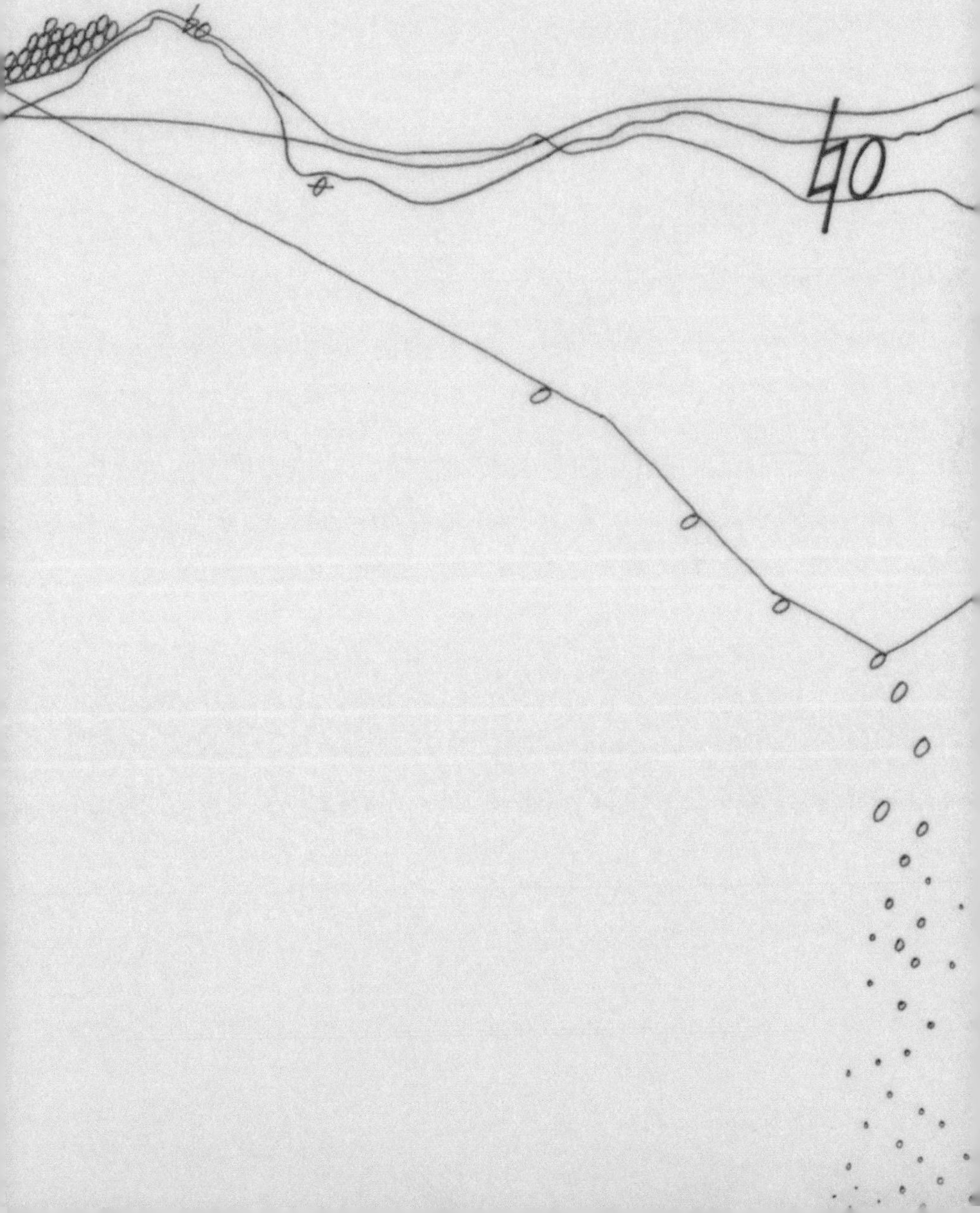
40

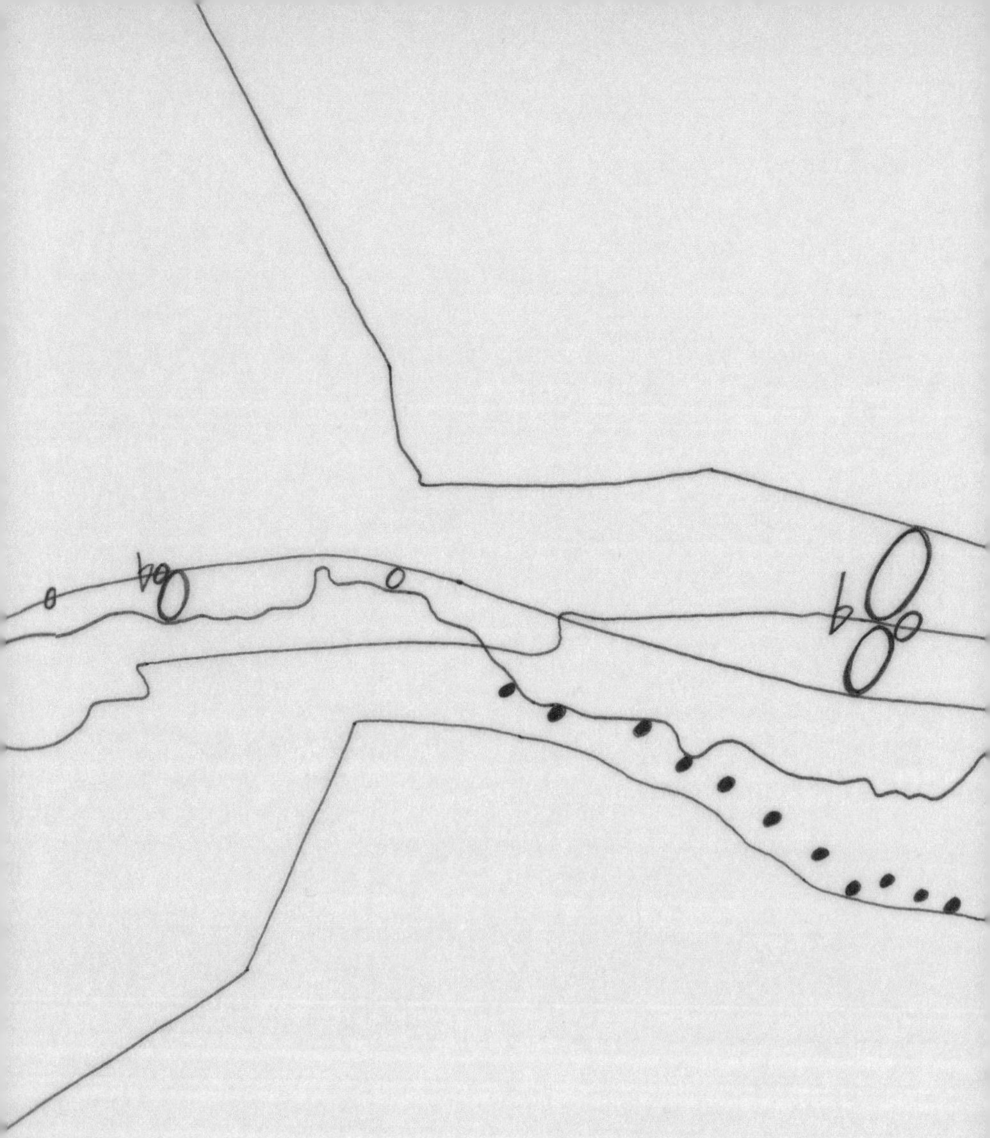

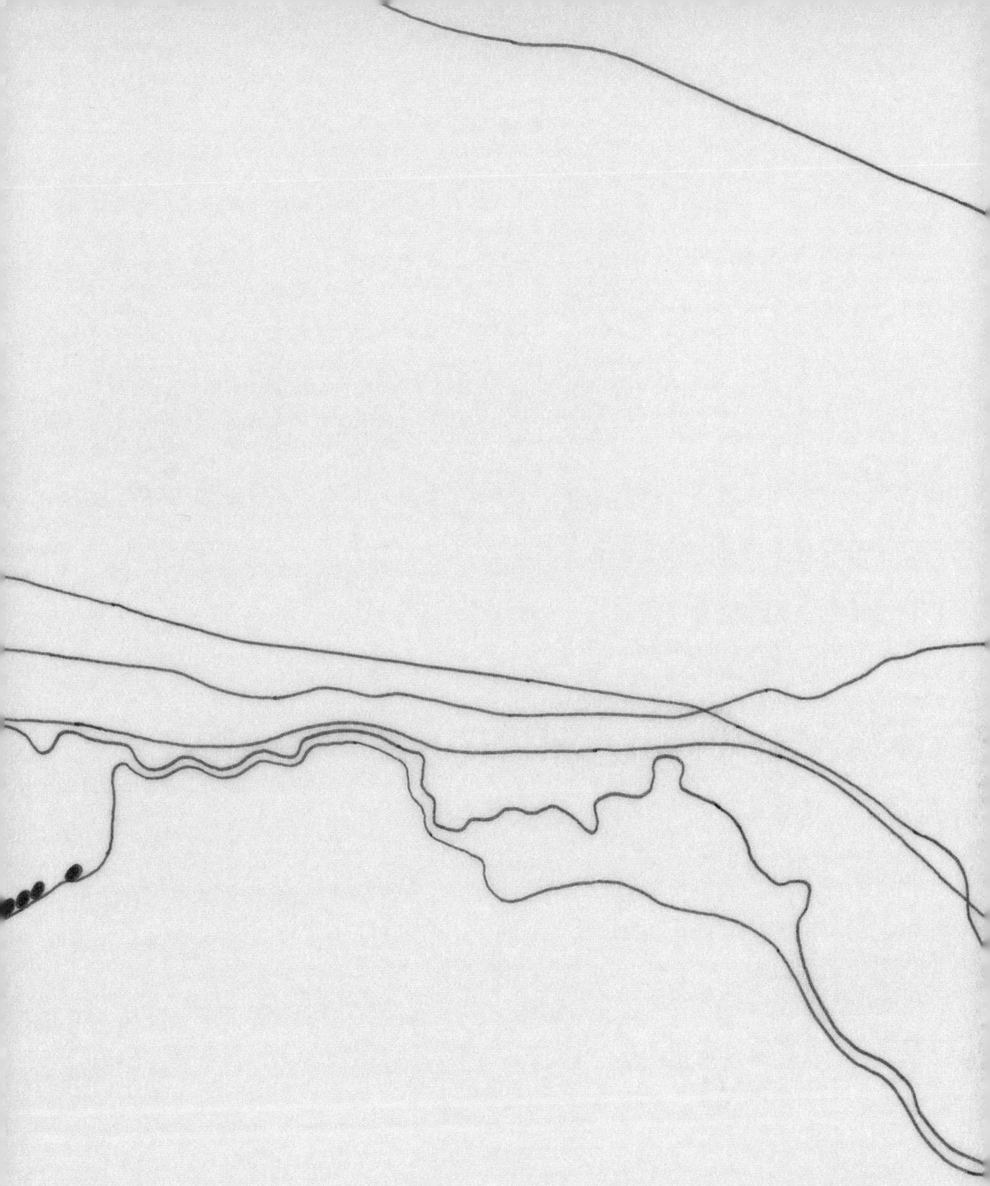

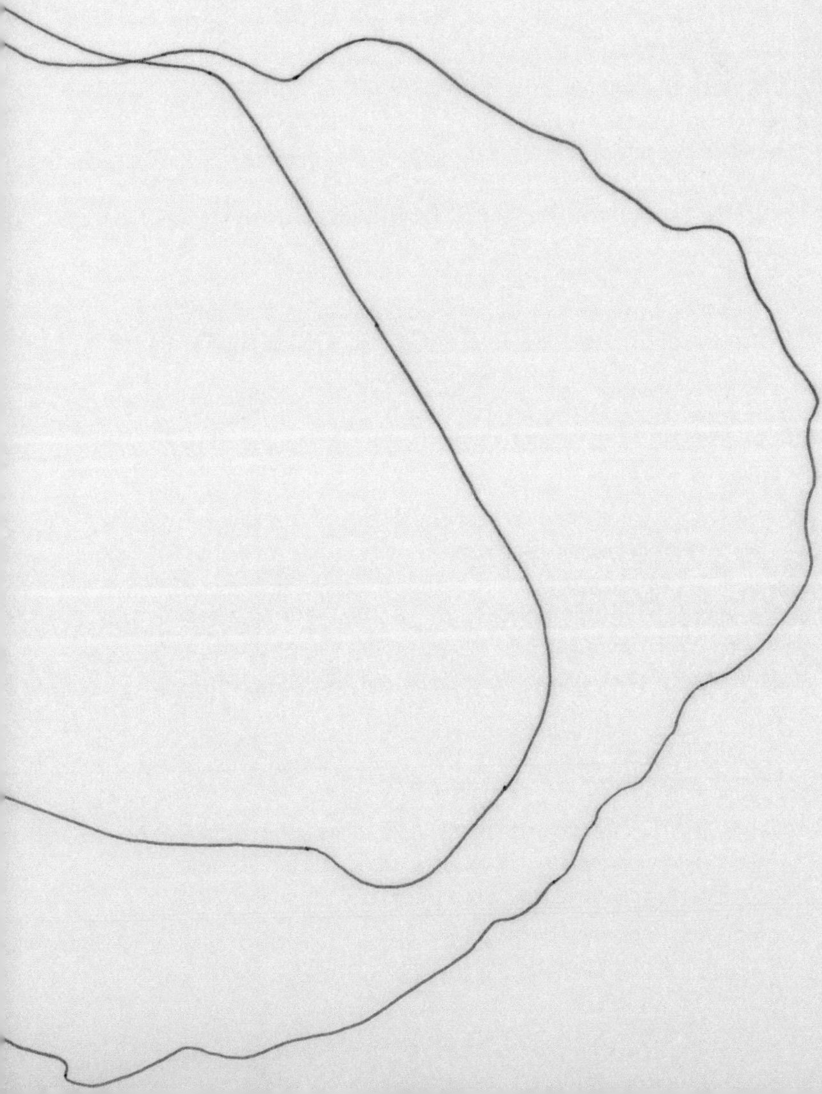

Looking & Listening

Is it the absence of one aspect of our sense of the Kentish landscape we are traversing, namely its sounds, that allows our thoughts to wander so freely when gazing out of the train window?

This is how the philosopher Jean-Luc Nancy describes listening:

> "If 'to hear' is to understand the sense (either in the so-called figurative sense, or in the so-called proper sense: to hear a siren, a bird, or a drum is already each time to understand at least the rough outline of a situation, a context if not a text), to listen is to be straining toward a possible meaning, and consequently one that is not immediately accessible.
>
> We listen to someone who is giving a speech we want to understand, or else we listen to what can arise from silence and provide a signal or a sign, or else we listen to what is called 'music'. In the case of these first two examples, one can say… that listening strains toward a present sense beyond sound. In the latter case, that of music, it is from sound itself that sense is offered to auscultation.
>
> …To be listening is always to be on the edge of meaning…
>
> …To be listening is to be *at the same time* outside and inside, to be open *from* without and *from* within…"[1]

And for Steven Connor there is a distinct difference between hearing and seeing the world:

> "When we see something, we do not think of what we see as a separable aspect of it, a ghostly skin shed for our vision. We feel that we see the thing itself, rather than any occasion or extrusion of the thing. But when we hear something, we do not have the same sensation of hearing the things itself… We hear, as it were, the event of the thing, not the thing itself."[2]

And here on this train these sonic events of your imagination mingle with the things you see. Here's Georges Perec:

> "We use our eyes for seeing. Our field of vision reveals a limited space, something vaguely circular, which ends very quickly to left and right, and doesn't extend very far up or

down. If we squint, we can manage to see the end of our nose; if we raise our eyes, we can see there's an up, if we lower them, we can see there's a down. If we turn our head in one direction, then in another, we don't even manage to see completely everything there is around us; we have to twist our bodies round to see properly what was behind us.

Our gaze travels through space and gives us the illusion of relief and distance. That is how we construct space, with an up and a down, a left and a right, an in front and a behind, a near and a far.

When nothing arrests our gaze, it carries a very long way. But if it meets with nothing, it sees nothing, it sees only what it meets. Space is what arrests our gaze, what our sight stumbles over: the obstacle, bricks, an angle, a vanishing point. Space is when it makes an angle, when it stops, when we have to turn for it to start off again. There's nothing ectoplasmic about space: it has edges, it doesn't go off in all directions, it does all that needs to be done for railway lines to meet well short of infinity."[3]

1 Jean-Luc Nancy, *Listening* (New York: Fordham University Press, 2007) pp.6–14.

2 Steven Connor, 'Edison's Teeth: Touching Hearing' in V. Erlmann (ed.), *Hearing Cultures: Essays on Sound, Listening and Modernity* (Oxford/New York: Berg Publishers, 2004) p.157.

3 Georges Perec, *Species of Space and Other Pieces* trans. John Sturrock (London: Penguin, 2008) p.81.

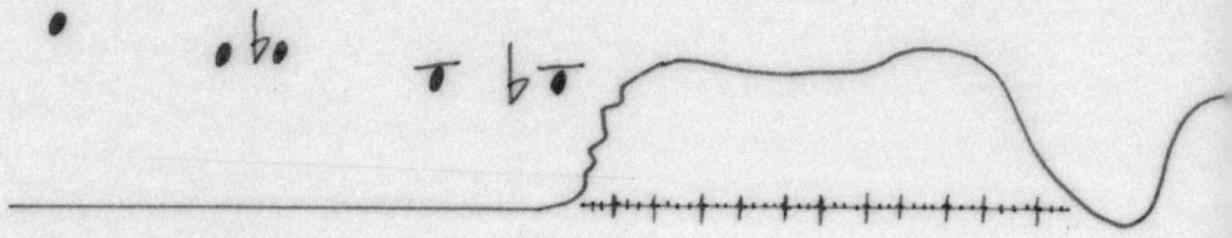

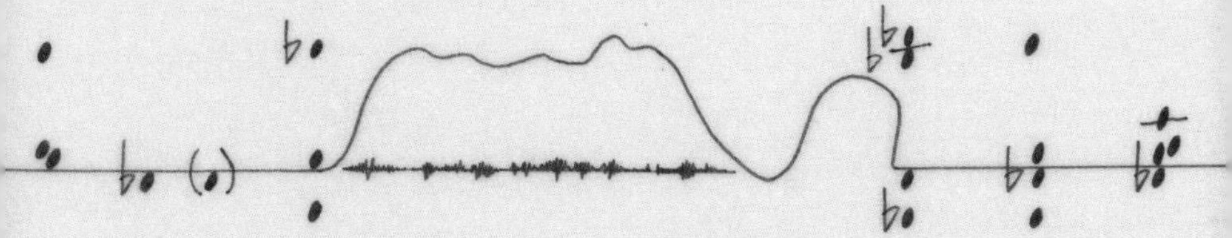

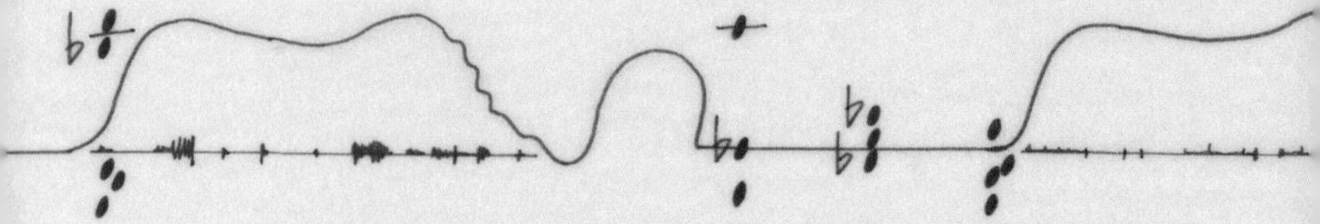

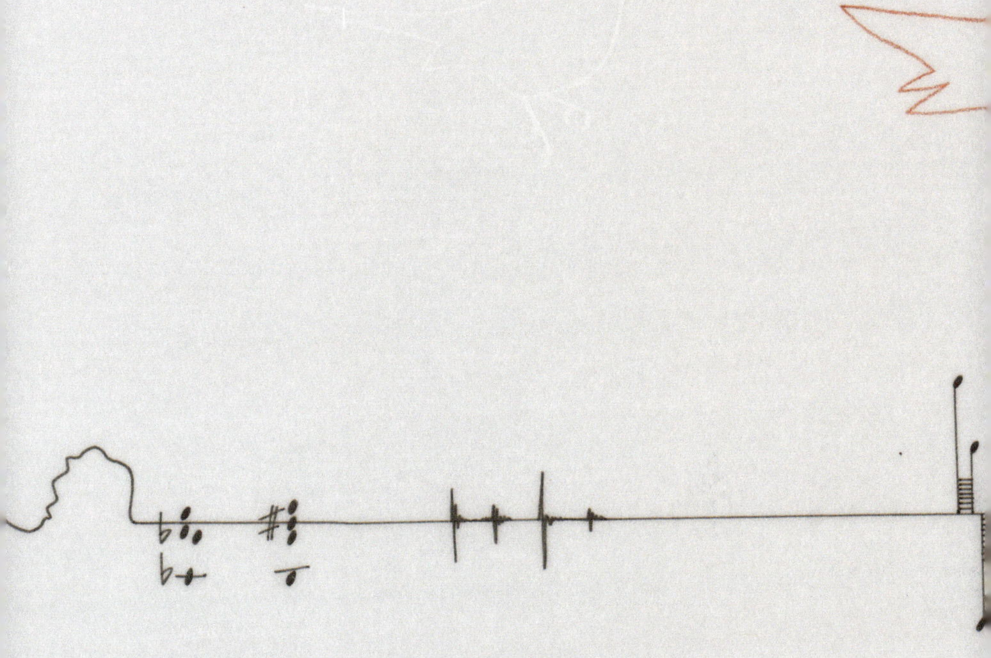

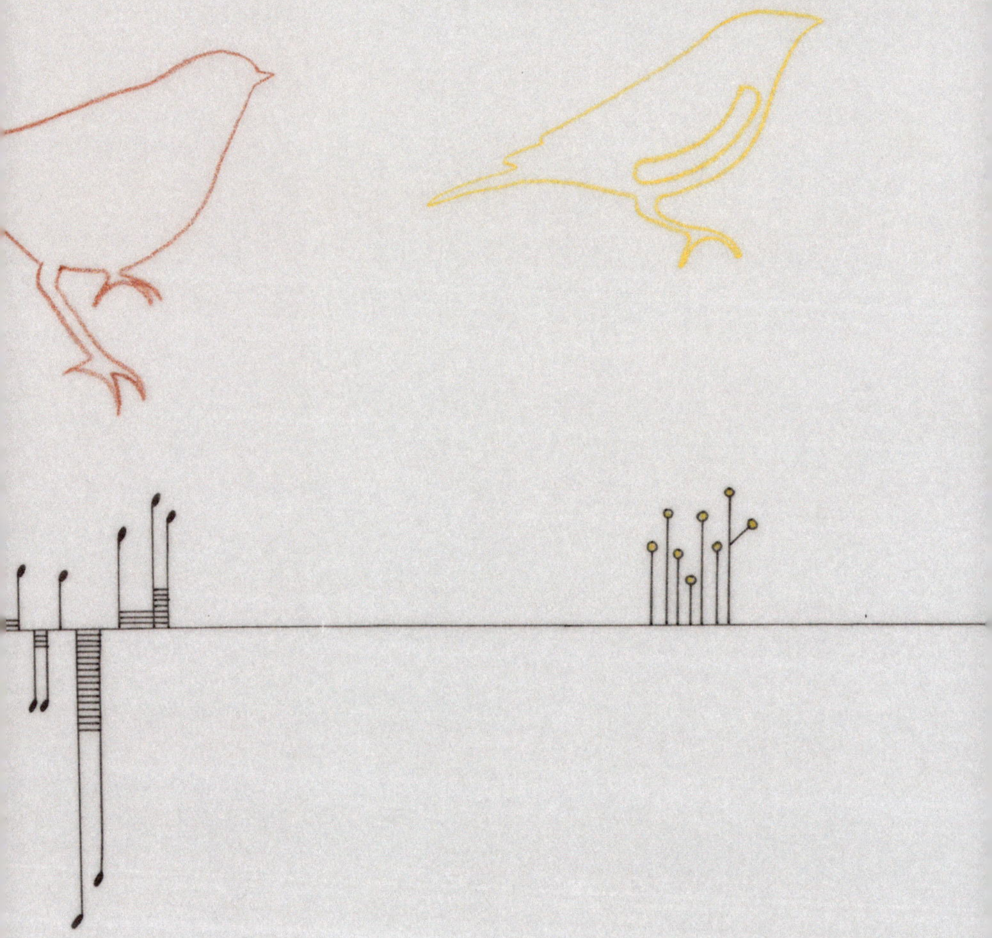

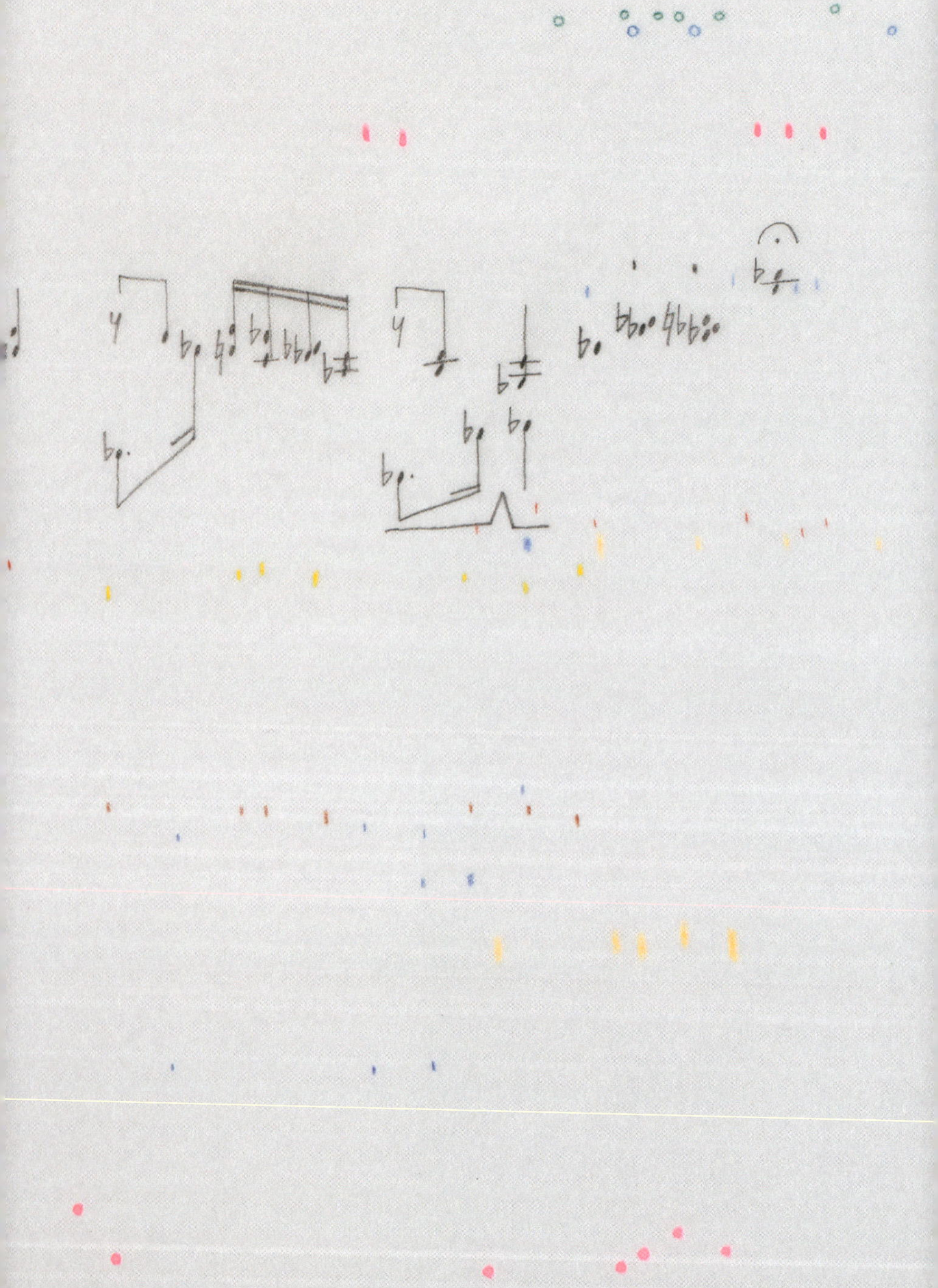

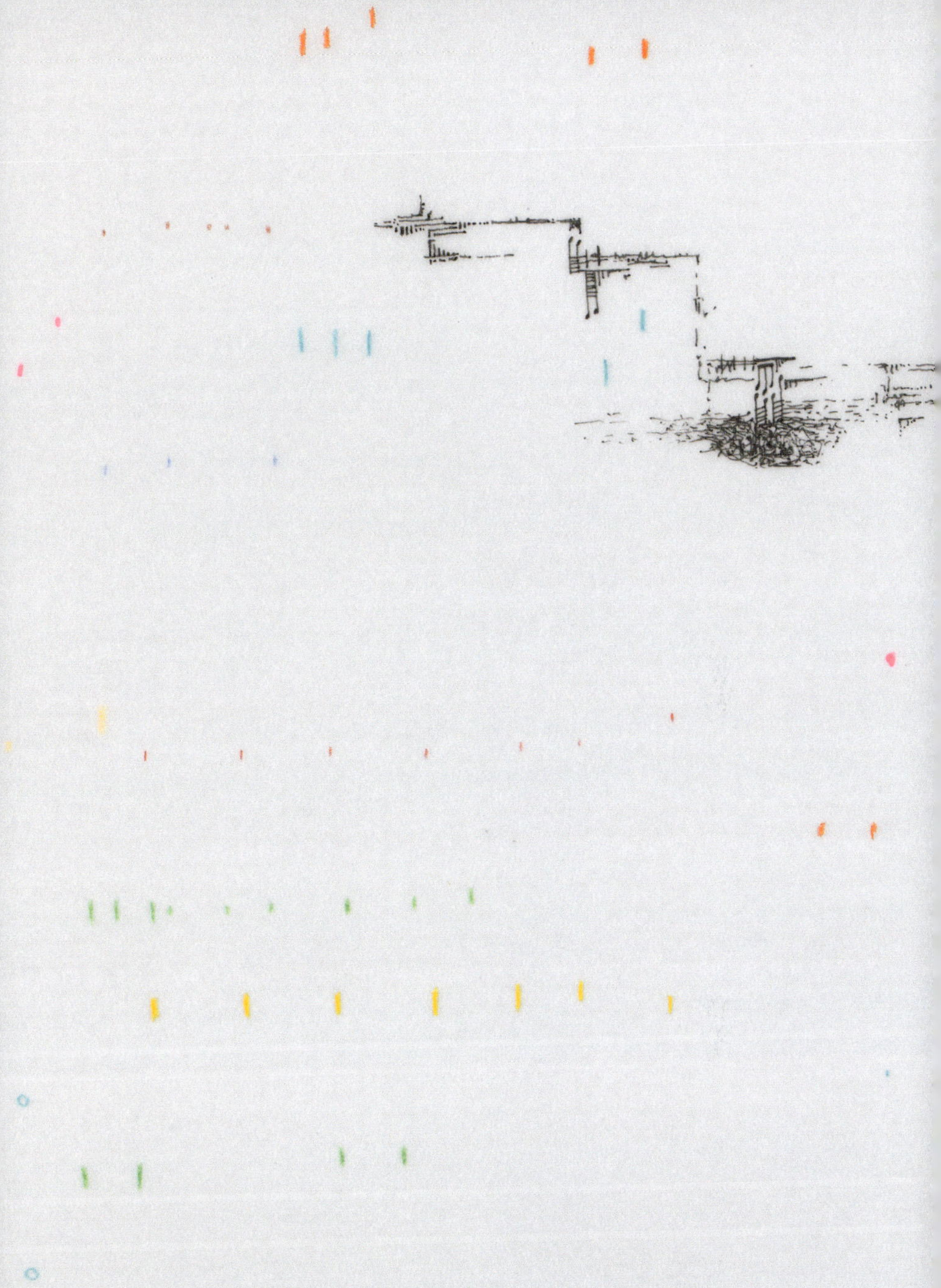

Sonorama

1. St Pancras to Ebbsfleet

All Aboard for Margate

Recording from the British Library archive, 1905, sung by Florrie Forde.

Tunnel Waltz

Composed and recorded by Claudia Molitor including a field recording by by Jay-Dea Lopez.

Night on London's River

Recording from BBC sound archive, 1933, spoken by Gerald Cock.

Thames Suite

Composed and recorded by Claudia Molitor including a field recording by Peter Toll.

Reading 1: Railway

With quotes from: Charles Dickens *Household Words*, 1851. Paul Farley and Michael Symmons Roberts *Edgelands: Journeys into England's True Wilderness*, 2012. Filippo Tommaso Marinetti, translated by Jeffrey T. Schnapp, in J. T. Schnapp(ed.) *Speed Limits*, 2009. Wolfgang Schivelbusch *The Railway Journey: The Industrialization of Time and Space in the 19th Century*, 1986. L. M. Evans *Navvies and Their Needs*, 1878.

Read by Sara Mohr-Pietsch, Tim Meacham, Conal McStravick, Ain Bailey, Irene Revell, Maria Chavez.

2. Ebbsfleet to Ashford

The Crane: Quayside Dreaming

Composed and recorded by Claudia Molitor including a field recording by Lawrence Shove.

Reading 2: Journeying

With quotes from: Rebecca Solnit *A Field Guide to Getting Lost*, 2006. Tim Ingold *Lines: A Brief History*, 2007. Rainer Maria Rilke, in a letter to a friend, 1923.

Read by Amber Priestley, Sara Mohr-Pietsch, Irene Revell, Maria Chavez.

Pylon Murmurings

Composed and recorded by Claudia Molitor.

Evan Parker & Graham McKenzie

In conversation at Turner Contemporary, Margate.

3. Ashford to Canterbury

Interlude 1

Composed and recorded by Claudia Molitor.

Subterranean Histories

Composed and recorded by Claudia Molitor including a field recording by by Nigel Tucker.

Reading 3: Hop picking

With quotes from: John Christopher and Simon Jeffs (eds.) *Bradshaw's Guide: Vol.4: South Eastern Railway: London, Chatham & Dover*, 2014. George Orwell in P. Davidson (ed.), *The Orwell Diaries*, 2009. Recordings of 'Opping Holiday' BBC interview with hop pickers in 1934, Nelson Ridley 'The Hop Picking Tragedy', Ray Driscoll 'Hopping down in Kent'.

Read by Sara Mohr-Pietsch, Conal McStravick, Amber Priestley.

Woodland Variations, no.14

Composed and recorded by Claudia Molitor including a field recording by Richard Margoschis and Phill Riddett.

Interlude 2

Composed and recorded by Claudia Molitor.

4. Canterbury to Ramsgate

Stour-Rhine

Composed and recorded by Claudia Molitor.

Reading 4: Looking & Listening

With quotes from: Jean-Luc Nancy *Listening*, 2007. Steven Connor, 'Edison's Teeth: Touching Hearing' in V. Erlmann (ed.) *Hearing Cultures: Essays on Sound, Listening and Modernity*, 2004. Georges Perec *Species of Spaces and Other Pieces*, trans. John Sturrock, 2008.

Read by Sara Mohr-Pietsch, Tim Meacham, Ain Bailey, Conal McStravick.

Bird Song

Composed and recorded by Claudia Molitor including a field recording by Jay-Dea Lopez and Phil Riddett.

Reflections on Roman Kent

Charlotte Higgins in conversation with Claudia Molitor and Irene Revell at Richborough Roman Fort.

5. Ramsgate to Margate

Die Muschel von Margate

Music by Kurt Weill, text by Felix Gasbarra. Recording by Angelina Reaux with Robert Kapilow.

In Celebration of Immigration

'Immigration RSVP', a poem by, and read by, Lemn Sissay. Music composed by Claudia Molitor. Performed by Jan Hendrickse (flutes).

A CONVERSATION WITH CHARLOTTE HIGGINS

Reflections on Roman Kent

CLAUDIA MOLITOR: In your book *Under Another Sky: Journeys in Roman Britain* (2014) you mention that you actually walked certain Roman roads, rather than simply driving from ruin to ruin. Was approaching these Roman remains on foot important to you?

CHARLOTTE HIGGINS: Yes, I think that was really important. It was partly borne out of necessity, because I don't have a car, but there's something about discovering the landscape at a walking pace that is interesting. And for me personally it felt like a bit of a release moving toward things quite slowly, and just nice to be outside in nature as well. Sometimes it's rather scrappy nature, because Roman remains are not always in incredibly scenic spots; through wasteland or through semi-industrial spaces or even along dual carriageways.

CM: And when you were walking did you ever imagine how it must have been for Romans at that time? Did you imagine how the landscape might have sounded, smelt or looked differently?

CH: I always found it really difficult to empathise my way into being Roman, partly because I feel so strongly the impossibility of doing that. I think I was always very aware of myself approaching these ancient remains, 2000 years on, walking through a landscape that had been encroached upon, changed, that wore its wrinkles as it were. Layer and layer of change visited upon it and yet in some sense these traces of antiquity had remained constant in this ever-changing landscape. So I never had that thing of "oh I'm a Roman centurion with a backpack on my back talking Latin", I just couldn't do that. It felt to me more like I was walking in the footsteps of a lot of other people who had had encounters with Roman Britain in one way or another, whether that was the Romans themselves encountering the landscape, or actually perhaps more closely those people who tried to understand the remains of Roman Britain before me: 18th century antiquarians, archeologists, the people who'd lived around what might be extremely confusing or strange traces of antiquity before they were understood for what they were. I was trying to find my way through all the mist of all this memory and the meaning that had accreted like archeological layers over the landscape.

CM: You mention in your introduction to your book that you wanted to explore how this Roman history remains latent in our sense of identity.

CH: British Roman history is a 400 year period in British history i.e., an extremely long period. In British notions about identity and history, it occupies a peculiar position for all kinds of reasons. It's partly because the Roman period seemed—although there are many opposing views on this both historically and anthropologically—to end very abruptly. There's no sense of continuity between the Roman period and what eventually becomes England, the Saxon period. There's this absolute disjunct. So that's one thing that I find fascinating. I wanted to reconnect with this very long period of British history.

In various periods, people have thought about Roman history very differently. In the 16th century, scholars were thinking about and rediscovering classical texts, making sense of them and using them to help them understand their own history. There's a sense that you can start thinking properly about Britain's history using these classical historians as your guide, rather than essentially making it all up in a wonderful welter of mythology, which is what had previously happened. If we had been scholars having this conversation in the late 16th Century then we'd have been talking enthusiastically about what connects us to the Romans and how Britain's Roman history was extremely important, and we'd have been talking about how it's the one thing that really allows us to winnow out myth and story from what actually happened. The great revelation of William Camden, who was the guy who really got this thinking going, was that there are these mysterious ancient monuments in the landscape, which people know about but perhaps understand imperfectly. On the other hand, there are all these extraordinary classical texts, relatively newly discovered accounts of Roman Britain, and you can tie these two things up and learn something about the country and its history and its landscape. So at that point in history the feeling of connectivity to the Romans was much, much greater.

Similarly, in the 18th century there was a sense of connection between Britain and its Roman past because these antiquarian traditions that William Camden got going were still developing.

There's an investment in this idea of the Romans having civilised Britain, and us good 18th century gentlemen being absolute inheritors of that civilising and scholarly tradition. But things get a little different in the 19th century, not least because we get a German Royal Family and it suddenly seems important and interesting to think about our Germanic roots and to start thinking about the origins of what is going to become our parliamentary democracy as being rooted in Anglo-Saxon traditions. There's this whole sense that Britain really starts when the Anglo-Saxons come, and Roman Britain gets slightly shunted off, historiographically speaking, into a corner, and the Romans are also associated with Catholic Italy… we're wandering off, is anyone keeping an eye on the footpath?

.

CH: It gets very complicated in the 19th century. On the one hand Britain is acquiring an Empire and the obvious model for that is the Roman Empire, and all the British Imperial administrators are learning the Classics at school and being inculcated in the notion of the virtuous Roman leader and so on. On the other hand, Britain was very much on the losing side as far as the Roman Empire is concerned, and obviously presents a model of the colonised rather than the colonising nation. The other complicated thing is that the late 19th century culture gets quite excited about figures like Boudica and Caractacus, who were ancient British heroes fighting off the Romans—ultimately unsuccessfully—but with great nobility and bravery. But on the other hand, we only know about these British heroes because the Romans wrote about them—there's no other corroborating evidence even that they ever existed. You have the sense that there are these brave but ultimately defeated Iron Age British characters; and they only really exist in the imagination because the Romans might have invented them, or at least invented their literary and historical characters.

IRENE REVELL: Was there ever an attempt, in the intervening centuries, to maybe claim a coherence between the Romans and the British, or that we are Roman?

CH: Yes, there was that, but it was unsuccessful in the end. One thing that happened, for example, which is perhaps not quite what you're suggesting but the opposite of that, is that Boudica was co-opted as a precursor to Queen Victoria. So you do get this intriguing notion that when there is a female ruler in Britain, there aren't a great number of precursors, so you cast back into history and eventually you get to Boudica, or Boadicea as she's more often known. The name Boadicea means victory, so that obviously reminds you of the name Victoria, and there's a reason there's a great statue of Boadicea in her chariot with her daughters, being rushed forward by these magnificent horses on Westminster Bridge by the Houses of Parliament: it's an open reference to Queen Victoria. The horses are modeled on Prince Albert's horses, and it was erected just after Queen Victoria died, which is also incredibly troubling because Boudica lost and Boudica was not only noble, but incredibly violent and practically a terrorist, a war criminal of extraordinary brutality, slaughter. So to me it never quite settles down, and this is what makes Roman Britain history so interesting, it complicates rather than comforts.

CM: You mention the idea of the Romans having civilised the indigenous Brits. Was this a cultural civilisation?

CH: Yes, there's a very clear passage in the Agricola by Tacitus, the Great Roman historian. The Agricola is the biography of Agricola, the governor of Britain, and Tacitus' father-in-law. It's actually a very good source because he had great access to his father-in-law who was a very important figure in Roman Britain's history. There is a passage in which Tacitus says that, by-and-by, the aristocratic Iron Age Britons began to take on all the manners and mores of the Roman aristocracy and they built porticos and baths and installed underfloor heating, and spoke Latin, and began to throw delicious dinner parties. So it's absolutely cultural, and embedded in that passage that I've paraphrased very loosely is the sense that becoming Roman, becoming civilised, is about habit and manner, is about doing things that are Roman. You can become Roman if you have the right architecture, the right manners, if you eat the right food, if you speak the right language and if in fact you have the right religion—if you do the right things in relation to Roman gods—then you can become Roman. This passage is a very short but intriguing paragraph and is very much latched onto in later readers of Tacitus. It's very important for William Camden who's writing in the late 16th century, and it's very important in the 18th century, where the gentleman antiquarians who are thinking about Roman Britain are very invested in the idea of manners and politeness, which of course was a topic of considerable interest in that era that 'discovers' manners and polite behaviour.

The interesting thing about this passage for me is the tone, as there is something slightly ambiguous or sarcastic about it. I think the suggestion is that this is not a wholly positive thing, that something has been lost in the process, and that taking on these very Roman ways of life is not necessarily all for the good; it's not absolutely a one-way brilliant process. Tacitus was quite invested in the notion that Rome is decadent, that Rome isn't quite what it used to be, Rome is corrupt, and you get a sense in his writing that the further out from the centre of the Empire you go, the more authentic, in a sense, the people are: the less corrupt, the less wealthy, the more noble. In a curious way, he has an odd relationship with Britain, because Britain is absolutely on the edge of the Roman Empire, and the British people are absolutely the poorest people you could come across. But in a sense that renders them free of these perhaps rather baleful influences that are present in the centre of the Roman Empire. So perhaps they lose a bit of that when they start to become a bit more Roman.

CM: What's interesting about that is that you have a society that at some point was looked at by others as still having this pure, natural state, which of course comes with its problem of exoticising and making 'other'. But then, later in its history, Britain becomes really prolific in doing exactly that to others, of exoticising other countries.

CH: Absolutely, you get the sense that the Romans exoticised the ancient Britons, and then the Britons do that themselves, many hundreds of years later. And you can see this in the earliest colonial adventures of Britain in the 16th and 17th centuries to the Eastern seaboard of what is now the USA. Early ethnographers made these rather wonderful, slightly troubling drawings of people living in America, and they look exactly how they imagined ancient Britons. So there's a sense that the, as-it-were, 'primitive' people of Iron Age Britain were quite similar to the 'primitive' people of the Americas. Those British people who were chronicling the people they encountered in America, native Americans: their model for understanding them were ancient Roman accounts of British people.

·

CH: I suppose what I find bewitching about this place [Richborough Fort] is the sense that this bit of Kent really is the place where exits and entrances, *national* exits and entrances, have been made, and it feels like it's been the point of arrival for wave after wave of people arriving in Britain. The Romans were just one layer: the Celts would have arrived at some point in the deep past, and then the Romans, the Saxons, the Normans, and so on. Very close to here there was a huge refugee camp during the Second World War for young male Jewish refugees from continental Europe. It feels to me very much like a gateway into Britain. I suppose the other thing I really love about this place is that the landscape has changed so much—so that when you stand here you can see this enormous industrial complex which is the old pharmaceuticals factory, and if you look in the other direction you can see where there used to be an old power station. You're looking out over seas of grass, as well as industry. There is a sort of rural feeling to it and at the same time you can always hear the pounding away of the A road. For the Romans, it would have been surrounded on three sides by water. It would have been a very busy port. It's kind of hard to imagine the cacophony of voices of all nations because the Roman army would have been made up of people from all over the Roman Empire: from Libya, Syria, Hungary, Germany; people talking Latin in different accents; British people talking in funny accents, or amongst themselves in their own language.

IR: It still feels sort of incongruous this Roman fort.

CH: Yes, it feels like it's been plonked into the landscape.

IR: Which it must have done in Roman times too?

CH: It certainly would have done. There is that sense that one often feels with Roman remains—perhaps not maybe so much when you're actually in Rome, but Roman remains in other parts of the Roman Empire—that they're so geometrical. We are in a world of straight lines and uniformity, and they are *standardised* so we could be in Syria and stand in a Roman fort and we would, having learned the way this fort arranges itself, have the barracks in the centre and the camp commanders head quarters in another part of it. All of that is completely standardised in the Roman Empire wherever you go. There is a sense of utter familiarity but at the same time something very incongruous about these objects in the landscape. And it feels quite different from when you walk into the ruins of a Norman monastery, for example.

IR: I guess it reflects that sense you were talking about earlier, that it never really got taken up into British culture in the same way that Saxon history did.

CH: There's often a sense that it is cut off and there's a lack of continuity. Though that doesn't always apply actually: at Pevensey fort, which is in Sussex, just round the coast from here, there is a very strong sense that this place has always been used, because it got converted into a medieval castle, and it was fortified when the Armada was on its way. It was refortified extraordinarily in the Second World War with gun emplacements built into the medieval keep, which itself is encircled by Roman walls. In that sense, there really is a continuity. But often you get these great military installations having been left stranded in the landscape: they were of no use after the Romans were gone. In the case of this fort, Richborough, there is a little Saxon chapel huddled into the corner of the fort, which feels very much like an afterthought.

CM: The fort was left behind because it didn't have any function anymore and the power station that you mentioned was decommissioned, the pharmaceutical plant is being abandoned—this part of England seems very fluid, constantly changing.

CH: Very much so. The idea of Kent not being static and always changing, always fluctuating, to me connects with the sense of it being where people come in, and where people go out. It's always been moulded and changed by the people who come here. It always seems to be on the sharp end of change somehow. The thing that fascinates me is that Kent is thought and known about by the Romans; it's the first part of Britain to be named as a separate entity within the whole idea of Britain. Diodorus Siculus, who was a Roman from Sicily writing in Greek, wrote a description of Britain where he mentions Kantium [in 1st century BC]. It's really startling when you read this: I mean it's in Greek and broadly of the period of Julius Caesar, and he writes about Kantium, Kent. And you realise it's *still* called Kent. That's such an extraordinary degree of continuity in a way.

For those historians and ethnographic writers in Roman times there was, as we've already discussed, this intriguing notion that the closer you got to Rome geographically, the more civilised you were, and that counted within Britain as well. So Kent was definitely the most civilised part of Britain because it was nearest the continent. They had more access to Roman ways of behaving and clearly there was more traffic between Roman Gaul, the Romanised world generally and this particular part of Britain. Again you get this sense that there was a lot of exchange going on even before the Romans formally conquered Britain in 43 AD. The local elites of this part of Britain were already evolved in the Roman world: they were importing delicious olive oil and drinking wine. This sense that Kent was almost touching continental Europe was very strong I think.

Charlotte Higgins was born in Stoke-on-Trent and studied Classics at Balliol College, Oxford. She is *The Guardian*'s chief culture writer and author of *Under Another Sky: Journeys in Roman Britain*.

EVAN PARKER & GRAHAM McKENZIE

Looking & Listening

GRAHAM McKENZIE: Okay, so now Evan and I are in the harbour café looking out at the sea at Margate. We've just come down on the train earlier and we're going to have a little chat now about looking and listening. As someone working in free music and free improvisation, amongst other genres, you are often in a situation where people observe this from the outside. Perhaps there's a lot going on, on the stage, very often you may be in a situation where you're performing with people for the first time, or maybe you've not performed with on too many occasions. In terms of you being on the stage, how important is listening to and also observing what's going on around you?

EVAN PARKER: Yes, well, this might be slightly disappointing for the theme we're talking about—once I start to play I shut my eyes, unless I'm reading music, which would usually be someone else's music—and that's pretty much a rarity for me these days, so when I'm improvising I shut my eyes, so I don't know what I'm actually seeing—maybe inner visions.

The theme immediately made me think of a piece that John Stevens wrote in the very early days of what you could call the transition from free jazz to free improvisation. Most of the players that John was working with came out of a modern jazz background, but we were on the cusp of moving towards something much more open. These days people are coming from all kinds of backgrounds, not necessarily a jazz background, because they find the notion of open improvisation or free improvisation to be quite attractive and welcoming. Back then I think John had to explain his ideas more carefully. The title of this discussion—looking and listening—made me think of that piece he wrote called 'Seeing Sounds and Hearing Colours'—it was of course the days of LSD in the water supply and I can't say for sure that John wasn't somehow inspired by a psychedelic experience, but that was the title of the piece. With that whole business of synaesthesia, some people have more pronounced effects. I think Scriabin was famous in that synaesthetic way—he had a table of correspondences between pitches and colours. I have to say I don't have that faculty, and when I'm looking, I'm looking and when I'm listening, I'm listening. The thing about improvising is that you have to listen very carefully to everything that's going on—it's listening and psychoanalysing that's appropriate as a theme for group improvisation because you have to know or read the emotional and psychological significance of particular gestures from other players, particularly players that you know well because they can help you to structure the bigger form. The moment-to-moment form is not so difficult, but somehow there has to be a faculty that is also taking care of the overall form: how long are we going to play, how long is this piece going to be? There are some guidelines like that at the beginning of a piece, but very often the cues are all internal and, to an extent psychological, so it's not really listening to, it's more analysing, psychoanalysing the other players.

GM: You talked about John Stevens, and John perhaps having to explain his ideas a bit more. I wonder if you feel that responsibility too?

EP: No, no, no, no—things have changed so much in the interim! Now there's a community of players at the highest levels in all the centres in Europe, in America or in Japan. There are really tremendous players who don't need anything explained, they're ready to play and polite enough to agree with your instructions if there is a framework that you have in mind. If it's your situation, you're in control, you're the employer for the moment. But in the community of players I work with we all effectively take it in turns to be the leader and to be playing the supporting role. As I say there's no comparison, the thing has really grown very fast, to be a worldwide phenomenon.

I should add it's a great shame that John didn't live long enough to pick the fruit of his labour, because he was one of the leaders and proselytisers. He took flack from more conventional jazz players because he was making waves. He was disturbing the scene a little bit, and never really got the appreciation he deserved. But his name will never go away: he has loyal fans like me that will never stop citing him as an influence. He was such an important supporter of what I was trying to do.

GM: As a little aside, talking about appreciation and John not being around... I was in Reckless Records on Berwick Street [in London] the other day, and I can't for the life of me remember which recording it was but there was a John Stevens LP which they were selling for £150 I think, and I wonder what you think John Stevens might think of his LPs now selling in Reckless Records for £150.

EP: He was a driven character, and the thing that often seems to be the case with people that die young is they pack more into the time they've got. John would get up early and stay up late, get a lot done every day, every day meet people, meet people you knew, meet people you'd never heard of, you never knew what the discussions were about but you always knew it was always moving something along to the next place. The whole Community Music project that he gave so much to meant a lot to him. Now people are starting to discover the work he did. There's an interest in pedagogy: the teaching of improvisation is now on the curriculum for a lot of places, all around those same areas we spoke about—North America, Europe, Japan... there are universities where you can go and study it.

GM: Is that something you approve of?

EP: Yeah I think it's great, it means there are people who want to do it. When you begin you need a protection from the real world, and I always think of academia—maybe naïvely—as a haven away from the real world. And that's a great situation when people are starting out.

GM: Don't you worry that this will result in academia setting rules for improvisation that perhaps didn't exist, a development of a right way and a wrong way to improvise?

EP: Well there are already signs of that kind of orthodoxy starting to become established. John's approach is in some ways the complete opposite of, say, Eddie Prévost's workshop but they each identified skills that need to be developed if you want to be involved in group improvisation. Their work should be recognised and historically prior to later efforts.

GM: I always think that if Monk went to Berkley now they'd tell him he was playing the piano wrong. I sometimes worry when things get too deep into the world of academia.

EP: That's the worst that can happen. The best that can happen is people use that protected time as a space to develop something that is then strong enough to survive on the outside. It's like a hothouse situation… harden the plants off in the greenhouse and then take them outside in the sun and the fresh air or, more realistically, the rain and the frost!

GM: Turning to the audience for a minute, and back maybe to looking in particular: often people will talk about free jazz, free improvisation, as very much a live experience rather than perhaps a recorded experience. People might acknowledge the recording as a document, and perhaps it's not something that you listen to in the way you listen recordings of other music. Do you think that's because, for the audience, free improvisation is a very visual experience as much as a listening experience? Does the audience feel a strong need to see what the musician is doing on stage?

EP: I think it probably helps that they're using other kinds of cues in addition to the pure sounds. They're using the body language of the players and what they can see as the interaction between the players as cues for understanding the music. But once they're familiar with the music perhaps they might start to listen with their eyes shut, I've got no idea. In the same way I play with my eyes shut, I very often listen with my eyes shut.

GM: I'm always extremely jealous of people who can do that. In some ways to shut out other things I very often want to close my eyes but I know I'll fall asleep. And it's no reflection on who's playing or any comment on my enjoyment of the concert, but if I'm sitting in a warm room and I'm listening to music and I close my eyes, that's it, I'm gone.

EP: But there's no more luxurious feeling than falling asleep at a concert of great live music. I mean it's nice to do it in bed as well when it's risk free. But that risk, the danger… the problem is the snoring… if you start to snore you've gone too far.

GM: I assume given that you play with your eyes closed, and you sit on stage taking a break from your playing, listening to what's going on around you… have you ever fallen asleep on stage?

EP: I've come very close to it… I can tell you a story, and I think under the circumstances Henry would forgive me identifying him. This was Henry Lowther, the fantastic trumpet player. We flew from

London to Vancouver, so there's already a time change that makes the day a lot longer. Midnight local time, Henry was involved in a small group concert and afterwards he told me he'd fallen asleep during his own solo—one of those so-called micro-sleeps, and I said, "well what happened?" and he said, "well, I woke up and I found myself playing a long note. So I just checked where we were and carried on." So you can actually fall asleep while you're playing, but I've never done that. I've come very close, but usually when there's written music and long periods when I'm not supposed to do anything.

GM: Do you think you go into a sort of trance onstage?

EP: Trance, what does it mean? You go into an altered state of feeling sometimes and you have all kinds of, I don't know what they are, delusions probably, but sometimes I have the feeling that I can breathe music, breathe in, inhale the music, and it's a very specific feeling. Trance: I suppose you have to be more or less on the edge of some special state to be able to think you can breathe music. After all you can't breathe music, it's a nonsense, so when you've got that feeling maybe you are already in an altered state.

.

EP: Art galleries tend to have very good acoustics and that becomes an important factor in the way it feels to play in those spaces. In fact I did a solo concert back in the summer upstairs [at Turner Contemporary], the room is very resonant to the point where certain frequencies were making one of the light fittings resonate. Then I've also done a concert downstairs with Matt Wright, in the space that overlooks the sea and that was deliberately timed for sunset so that as the sun set over the sea and the light in the gallery changed, gradually the emphasis switched from looking out of the windows to looking at video screens inside. But that was Matt's idea so I can't take too much credit for that. It was a very powerful atmosphere.

GM: That sense of nature, looking out at sea, or the change in natural light, does that influence what you're playing, even subconsciously? Are you responding to that in some way?

EP: "Subconscious in some way"—there's a lot of wiggle room in that! For the sake of being friendly I'll say yes, perhaps.

GM: I'll tell you a space that's interesting—again I wonder if you think people play differently—the Bimhuis in Amsterdam. In the new Bimhuis, you're sitting in the audience, and looking at the stage and then looking out at the city, the canals behind you… compared to the old Bimhuis, which was a darker clubbier environment. Certainly I feel it's a different experience as an audience member but as a musician do you think you're influenced at all?

EP: Speaking specifically of the Bimhuis, the story goes that the musicians asked the architect to reproduce the proportions of the old Bimhuis as closely as possible in the new building. Acoustically I've found the new building better than the old building, I find the whole situation there pretty much the best purpose-built jazz performance space in Europe.

GM: I was taken on a tour of the new Bimhuis, when they were building it. Sean Bergin was smoking two cigarettes at once and he was drinking, as was often the case, and he chucked some of his beer onto the wall, and he said to the person who was showing us around, "it has to smell the same as old Bimhuis"…

GM: You've played some really strange spaces. You told me once you performed in a septic tank?

EP: No, I played in an underground water storage tank somewhere in the outskirts of Zurich that was known to have a 20 second reverberation time. Pauline Oliveros has done several things in similar situations, she's the pioneer, of *deep listening*. I played solo in the Schlacht Turm, it's a monument to a particular battle outside of Leipzig with a very long reverberation time and I played solo there and of course when the acoustics are so markedly special then of course you have to play with the acoustics. There's no point in playing against them: they don't have a mind, they're just there, you have the possibility of working with them, they have only the possibility of being what they are, physically favourable to certain frequencies… Another remarkable one was the church that Markus Stockhausen had in Cologne, I don't know if he still has the use of the place, but it was a remarkable acoustic in the sense that the reverberation was so evenly distributed across the audible frequency spectrum that you didn't hear it when you were playing, only when you stopped. Not all big acoustics are like that, some are more present in your thinking, because they favour particular frequencies and you're looking to work the room in a literal sense, not work the audience but work the physical possibilities of the room.

There's a recording I made in a church in Chiswick that is dedicated to Michal Gerzon, the genius of live recording, 'Lines Burnt in Light'. That church had very specific, what you would call uneven resonance properties: it was almost as though you could place frequencies in different parts of the church and come back to them because they'd still be ringing, like a rhythmic cyclic visit to the different parts of the room, or in this case the church. It reminded me of the Theatre of Memory idea. Churches are useful in that way because of their good acoustics. They're built to make the vicar's voice powerful and the choir sound good, the organ sound good. You're often on a good thing with churches, sacred spaces. I think maybe one of the first times I went to Pisa I had that experience of going into the baptistry—the round building next to the famous leaning tower—and the guard there—I think it was a fairly standard thing—would demonstrate the acoustics by singing. There was an eight second reverberation time. Then I asked my friends in Pisa, can you arrange for me to do a concert there, and of course they were from the communist party, hard left, well-known atheists and the church in Italy is not so lenient. They quietly explained to me that the church still has a lot of power and influence in Italy and they don't want their buildings used for secular purposes. Whereas in England of course they're very happy for anything to be happening in a church, so I've benefited over the years from churches.

·

EP: On the theme of looking and listening I can talk a bit more about the late Roger Ackling who was an artist whose work I admired from the very first time I saw it. We became friends and we did a couple of performances of a piece that we constructed between us. We did it at the Cairn Gallery in Nailsworth. We decided to make something like the black monolith at the start of *2001*, but it also perhaps had something in common with a Punch and Judy show. It was a black box just big enough for the two of us to get inside, and some seats so people could watch. When the audience were in the room there was only the black box to be seen, then the lights went out and all hell broke loose in pitch dark. As soon as the lights went out Roger started to drill holes from inside the box. I came out of the box playing and turned slowly in a big circle around the box and back into the other side of the box, meanwhile Roger was drilling, drilling,

drilling, and then later came out of the box and was nailing, but all in the dark. After about forty minutes we both went back into the box, the drilling and banging stopped, the music stopped—it must have been very strange to experience. Immediately lights went on but only inside the box not outside, and through the holes that Roger had drilled came the star map of the sky above Nailsworth that evening. The many little nails he had painstakingly hammered in represented the Milky Way, the light shining on the heads of the nails was the Milky Way.

Roger was a great artist.

Evan Parker is a free-improvising saxophone player. Graham McKenzie is a writer, curator and Artistic Director of Huddersfield Contemporary Music Festival.

DAVID HENDY

Moving Echoes: tracking and evoking the lost sounds of the past

The sounds of the past always have to be imagined afresh. They can be guessed-at, plucked from the archives, recreated, evoked. Yet they can never be repeated. Or rather, they can never be repeated and *experienced* in precisely the same way as when first loosed upon the world. Even those sounds etched onto discs or magnetised on tapes turn out to be unreliable narrators. Where exactly were the microphones placed when trying to capture that passing train or those bleating sheep? What if they'd been pointing in the other direction? Would we have heard something altogether different? We'll never know. Microphones do what they're told. They hear. We humans shift focus, pick out some sounds, ignore others. We *listen*. Most of us know about the 'Cocktail Party Effect': our ability to concentrate, if only fleetingly, on that far more interesting conversation which is happening over the shoulder of the person chatting away in front of us right now. It's a misnomer, really. For the Cocktail Party Effect is something we experience almost every waking hour, as we work, we play or rest or travel. We filter out the hum of that air-conditioning unit, the unending percussion of a dripping tap, the crackle of fluorescent lighting. We zoom-in on the cry of a baby, some vaguely interesting voice, an unfamiliar noise in the garden—a fox? Cats fighting? A burglar?—or perhaps just those soothing sounds of trees swaying in the breeze, which for some reason we didn't notice at first. Or vice versa, of course. For it might just be impossible to enjoy those swaying trees if we can't shake-off that drip-drip-drip or that mechanical hum. They fester in our minds, loudly obscuring all other sonic pleasures on offer.

What we listen to—as opposed to what we hear—depends, really, on our disposition, our mood, what sort of day we're having, what bugs us, what doesn't, what's familiar, what's strange. The sound of a place—or indeed the sound of a journey from one place to another—will never be the same for everyone. We are not talking about some objective reality. This 'soundscape' will mutate from moment to moment, as we move through it, turning this way and that, alone with our thoughts and emotions and memories. A kaleidoscope of acoustic fragments, shifting constantly—cohering into meaningful patterns and then just as suddenly breaking apart into ambiguity and chaos. A kaleidoscope of experiences.

Best, I reckon, to resist the urge to make full sense of this—especially if we're having to contemplate, as I do for a living, the long-ago evanesced soundscapes of the distant past. Any account claiming to be objective and definitive will surely be spurious. As an historian I'm supposedly duty-bound to trade in facts—to get as close to 'the truth' of the past as possible. And I do honestly think we can grasp *some* of it—offer a few impressions that at the very least don't mislead horribly. But there's a lot of guessing going on. A lot of selectivity, too. The process—and the end result—will always be largely an act of imagination. I flick through the archives and written accounts. I read first-hand accounts—of life among the navvies who are busy building the railways in London and Kent, blasting and digging and hammering their way under rivers, through hillsides, across valleys; of the raucous jumble of train-carriages filled to overflowing with hop-pickers from the East End hurtling to the fields for the season; of the hooded Victorian bathing-machines being hauled up and down the beaches of Margate, waiting to preserve the modesty of swimmers as they dip their toes into the water and fill their lungs with the sea air; of the cries of exhilaration from day-trippers on the Dreamland rollercoaster.

These written accounts are the kind of sources that are almost never ostensibly *about* sound. They're about ordinary—and sometimes extraordinary—lives being lived, day-by-day. Their lack of self-conscious contemplation of sound *as sound* is why I like them so much. References to the heard-worlds of the past, if they do crop up, are mentioned only in passing; they have a spontaneous honesty. More often than not, the sounds have to be inferred from the context. Which is when the Cocktail Party Effect takes hold. What happens to catch *my* eye (or perhaps more accurately my inner ear, busy conjuring imagined sounds as I read) will be just a word or a sentence. It will hint, tantalisingly, at how the quality of a person's life was, if only for a fleeting moment, shaped more than anything else by the sounds all around—sounds that had a visceral, unavoidable, enveloping, *in-your-face* presence. Reading between the lines, it's clear there'd have been few moments of quiet in the life of a nineteenth-century railway navvy—except perhaps on a Sunday. As for the well-to-do train-travellers on the newly opened London-to-Margate line, they'd have paid a pretty penny to avoid the din of the Hop-Picker specials or the third-class carriages—though whether they had quite as much fun on their journey as the poorer folk is a moot point. Noise can be pleasurable as well as irritating—though generally only when you have some control over the volume dial or the off-switch. The fundamental truth is that the poor could rarely get away from noise, while the rich usually could. The poor were usually accused of *making* too much noise—of being simply too *loud*. The rich, meanwhile, extolled silence—even insufferable, claustrophobic silence—as a virtue. Conjure up the sound-worlds of the past, and I find that inequality is never far from the surface of things. Is the world outside our train-carriage window any different now?

Naturally, another reader will have been drawn to very different things in these texts. He or she will have constructed a subtly different sense of what it was like to be alive at a particular point in time and space. But in every case, in every act of imagination, eavesdropping on the sounds of the past puts us right in the thick of the action. Immersed in sound, we become not detached spectators, but fully implicated participants. We are, for a moment, right *there*—side-by-side—with our ancestors. History and Imagination and Empathy all become deliciously entwined.

David Hendy is Professor of Media and Communications at the University of Sussex. He wrote and presented *Noise: a Human History* (BBC Radio 4, 2013) and is working on a history of the BBC, which will be published to coincide with the Corporation's Centenary in 2022.

IRENE REVELL

Sonorama: On Given Co-ordinates

A six-figure Ordnance Survey reference gives a precise space co-ordinate to within 100 square meters: a little patch that the Javelin, or any train on High Speed 1, would square in just a few seconds.

In Nam June Paik's film *A Tribute to John Cage* (1973) the two men set about to perform and video record four movements of the latter's *4'33"* in separate locations on the island of Manhattan, the co-ordinates of each site picked using one of Cage's best known aleatory methods, the *I Ching*. Subsequently the performance begins on a street in Harlem; the second, third and fourth movements take place, respectively, in a non-descript river location, the popscene of Times Square and Downtown, Beekman Street. As the camera does not, nor perhaps could not, hide, the performance comes up against the limits of this 'neutral' method—the spatial co-ordinates may have been chosen at random, as interchangeable, yet this device reveals the inescapable weight of history and culture any given site holds—in 1970s Harlem, the physical reality of race and class, in particular, rub unmistakably into the modernist utopia of the 'open score'.[1]

By contrast the tracks of the railway line seem to leave nothing of the journey to chance, as static as the staves of the conventional music score. And yet each repeat of such a seemingly fixed journey separated by the passage of time—whether the staccato of the daily commute, or a revisiting decades later—reveals as much difference as it confirms familiarity. As David Hendy remarks elsewhere, our understanding of history can only ever be partial, fleeting and, situated by our own personal histories, as they are in relation to others. And yet how might a score, a composition bridge this fracture—at once static, yet multiversal?

The voice of Florrie Forde heralds us from more than a hundred years past into the work. A frantic female narrator with her intermittent imperative sub clauses, half inviting and half sternly shepherding: "—all aboard!... *so all aboard*!". From the very start a powerful underlying ambivalence about the past and the present.

1 This moment in the work is explored by Philip Gentry in his essay 'The Cultural Politics of *4'33"*: Identity and Sexuality', in *Tacet no.1: Who is John Cage?* ed. Matthieu Saladin (2012).

Sonorama is a singular work, yet fragmented in as much as it comprises these heterogeneous elements; the knotted web of relations reflects these complexities in a work that is both inherently collaborative in multiple registers, yet at moments highly personal —multiple points that diffract potential for identification.

These are compositions made for the particular physicality of the train, this train seat, an incessant joggle: the adrenalin of getting somewhere fast, newness, power; but then again a dehumanising jaunt, pulling into nausea at times, the 'apoplexic rapidity' referred to in the first *Reading*. There is an attendant rhythm throughout the recordings, and yet not without its countering: piano melody against the chordal refrain in *Stour-Rhine*; the berserk acid-house of *Bird Song*, birds pitted against the naturalised pip/pop of the stylus; unfamiliarity both exciting and unnerving, in *Tunnel Waltz* the bow perhaps a collapsing javelin, failing better each time.

Upon the Kentish entry a joyfulness recounters with accordion in *The Crane* (an instrument belonging to the composer's grandfather, doubtless with its own complex personal history)—a relief to have escaped from London in these increasingly frantic times? The pylons of the national grid are both ubiquitous to the route, and at once a general feature of British long-distance railway travel, and seemingly function as a pivot propelling the compositions backwards and forwards, the minimalist drone of *Pylon Murmurings* unties this composition with those before and after.

The cello is a constant companion—with the piano—and intimacy of the voice, that work alongside the sometimes perverse moments of textual humanity—"with a big swallow for beer", or the terrible tale unearthed by the Seegers, summarised "with an e–i–o– an e–i–o– an e–i e–i o", the radical impulse of the story's collection bringing a sprain of optimism.

The playback device, mobile phone, or tablet, with headphones is surely a distancing tactic that allows the traveller, the listener to gain their own position within these specific space-time co-ordinates, assuming more fully the role of journeyer, and most pertinently, performer, of these arbitrary yet specific moments. The score of the route can never be more than a partial reading of a set of co-ordinates. Perhaps what *Sonorama* offers is more a set of given co-ordinates to be attended to in the knowledge that there might be an infinite further set, as listener, performer and composer alike.

Irene Revell is Director of Electra. She is also visiting curator on the MA Sound Arts course at London College of Communication and a member of the Cinenova Working Group.

ACKNOWLEDGEMENTS

We would like to thank Bryony Bishop, Michael Bull, Jamie Buchanan and Hornby, Davina Christmas, Stephen Connolly, Max Dixon, Pieter Francois, Myah Chun Grierson and Mick Grierson, Kate Griffiths and Southeastern, Tom Harper, Erkki Huhtamo, Holly Ingleton, Monique Kent, Joseph Kohlmaier, Victoria Pomery, Ben Lane, Cathy Lane, Sarah Martin, Peter Meanwell, Leone Molitor, Nicola and Michael Molitor, Azam Mullick, Fiona Parry, Vicky Pitchers, Vanda Playford, Ryan Roberts, Andrew Shedden, Lawrence Shove, Salomé Voegelin, Richard Whitelaw, Andrea Zarza.

Quotations in the readings: John Christopher and Simon Jeffs (eds.) *Bradshaw's Guide: Vol.4: South Eastern Railway: London, Chatham & Dover*, copyright 2014 Amberley, used by permission of Amberley Publishing. Steven Connor, 'Edison's Teeth: Touching Hearing' in V. Erlmann (ed.) *Hearing Cultures: Essays on Sound, Listening and Modernity*, copyright 2004 Berg Publishers, used by permission of Bloomsbury Publishing. Ray Driscoll 'Hopping down in Kent', courtesy Gwilym Davies collection. Paul Farley and Michael Symmons Roberts *Edgelands: Journeys into England's True Wilderness*, copyright 2012 the authors. Tim Ingold *Lines: A Brief History*, copyright 2007 Routledge, used by permission of Taylor & Francis Books. Filippo Tommaso Marinetti, translated by Jeffrey T. Schnapp, in J. T. Schnapp(ed.) *Speed Limits*, copyright 2009 the author. Jean-Luc Nancy *Listening*, copyright 2007 Fordham University Press. George Orwell in P. Davidson (ed.), *The Orwell Diaries*, copyright 2009 Penguin. Georges Perec *Species of Spaces and Other Pieces*, copyright 2008 Penguin. Nelson Ridley 'The Hop Picking Tragedy', courtesy Ewan MacColl & Peggy Seeger collection. Wolfgang Schivelbusch *The Railway Journey: The Industrialization of Time and Space in the 19th Century*, copyright 1986 the author. Rebecca Solnit *A Field Guide to Getting Lost*, copyright 2006 Canongate Books. Kurt Weill and Felix Gasbarra *Die Muschel von Margate*, published by European American Music Corporation, used by permission of the Kurt Weill Foundation for Music, Inc.

CREDITS

Sonorama is curated and produced by Electra in partnership with Turner Contemporary and the British Library. With funding and support from Arts Council England, Southeastern, Kent County Council Arts Investment Fund, Hornby, University of Kent.

Collaborators
David Hendy (University of Sussex)
Irene Revell (Electra)
Cheryl Tipp (British Library)

Contributors
Jan Hendrickse
Charlotte Higgins
Graham McKenzie
Evan Parker

Readers
Ain Bailey
Maria Chavez
Conal McStravick
Tim Meacham
Sara Mohr-Pietsch (narrator)
Amber Priestley
Irene Revell

Sonorama is available from the App Store 19 June–13 September 2015.
App design by Strangeloop.

ELECTRA

Turner Contemporary
LOTTERY FUNDED ARTS COUNCIL ENGLAND
BRITISH LIBRARY
University of Kent School of Music and Fine Art
Kent County Council
southeastern
HORNBY HOBBIES